Advance Praise for *The Good Struggle*

"Badaracco has written a valuable book that examines the evolving fundamentals of leadership in a contemporary world filled with greater uncertainty and more intense market pressures. *The Good Struggle* compels readers to look within, find what they bring to the table, and reflect on how the challenges of leadership impact all our lives in a very personal way."

—Gail McGovern, President and CEO,
American Red Cross

"Joseph Badaracco defines the essence of success in building a business: Live with the reality one competes in, but never stop dreaming about what might be possible."

—Tom Stemberg, Managing General Partner,
Highland Consumer Fund; Chairman
Emeritus, Staples, Inc.

"Leading responsibly does not equate to leading successfully. It is indeed a 'struggle.' This book challenges the reader to develop the right path for the long term. If you want answers, don't read this book. But if you want the right questions to ask, then this is the ultimate reference book to read again and again."

—Ann Fudge, former Chairman and CEO,
Young & Rubicam Brands

"People who consider themselves leaders or aspire to leadership in today's complex world must read this book. Its message is powerful: True leadership is forged from the personal crucible of struggle, values, and choices that justify the risks and time spent being a leader."

—Ronald K. Machtley, President,
Bryant University

"In this book, Joseph Badaracco, with his marvelous insight, foresight, and understanding about leadership, poses vital questions for leaders. In these times of turmoil and uncertainty, leaders must face these questions head on."

—Kunio Nakamura, former President,
Panasonic Corporation

"Dealing successfully with VUCA—volatility, uncertainty, complexity, and ambiguity—is inescapable for successful leaders today in their struggle to make the best choices for their companies, for their people, and for themselves. *The Good Struggle* provides an approach for leading responsibly amidst all the diverging forces."

—Daniel Vasella, MD, former Chairman
and CEO, Novartis AG

THE GOOD STRUGGLE

THE GOOD

STRUGGLE

Responsible Leadership in an Unforgiving World

JOSEPH L. BADARACCO

Harvard Business Review Press

Boston, Massachusetts

The web addresses referenced in this book were live and correct at the
time of the book's publication but may be subject to change.

Library of Congress Cataloging-in-Publication Data

Badaracco, Joseph.
    The good struggle : responsible leadership in an unforgiving world /
Joseph L. Badaracco.
        pages cm
    ISBN 978-1-4221-9164-4 (alk. paper)
    1. Leadership. 2. Social responsibility of business. I. Title.
    HD57.7.B327 2013
    658.4'092—dc23

                                                             2013018295

The paper used in this publication meets the requirements of the
American National Standard for Permanence of Paper for Publications
and Documents in Libraries and Archives Z39.48-1992.

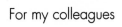

For my colleagues

Need and struggle are what excite and inspire us.

William James

What you spend years building, someone could destroy overnight. Build anyway.

Mother Teresa

CONTENTS

THE GOOD STRUGGLE

ENDURING QUESTIONS, EMERGING ANSWERS

In September 1961, a small plane crashed in the Congo and killed a Swedish diplomat named Dag Hammarskjöld—one of the most remarkable but little-known leaders of the last century. Hammarskjöld was a handsome, brilliant, well-connected man, at home in many languages and cultures. He could have had comfortable careers in banking, government, or academia. Instead, Hammarskjöld became a diplomat and the first secretary-general of the United Nations. The bold mandate of this unprecedented organization was preventing another world war and alleviating suffering around the globe. Hammarskjöld was on a dangerous peacekeeping mission when he died, and President Kennedy later hailed him as the greatest statesman of his century.

Hammarskjöld's other achievement was deeply personal. He kept a diary that gave a stunningly honest account of his inner life. This journal, which was later published with the title *Markings*, gives virtually no indication that its author was a successful, confident, accomplished leader. Instead, it is a chronicle of struggle and commitment in the face of profound uncertainty.[1] This perspective, I believe, is powerfully relevant today for understanding responsible leadership and for leading responsibly.

This may sound like a dispiriting view. Leadership, we hear so often, is about hopes and dreams, change and achievement, so why dwell on struggle? The answer is all around us. Struggle has always described leaders facing crises or strong resistance, but today a sense of anxiety and struggle has spread much further. It affects people throughout organizations and colors much of their experience. We live in an era of extraordinary opportunities for innovation, creativity, and social contribution, but uncertainty, intense performance pressure, risk, and turbulence also surround us. And the reason for the stunning opportunities and the widespread sense of struggle is one and the same: the market-driven world in which we live and work.

Markets now penetrate and shape almost every sphere of life. Almost everything—how we manage our organizations and our lives, how we make decisions at work and at home, and even how we think about ourselves—is deeply shaped by markets and market-based thinking.[2]

Markets—along with technological progress and sound government—have helped lift billions of people from grinding, dirt-floor poverty. They have provided a historically unprecedented level of material wealth to middle classes around the globe. But markets have also produced depressions, shocks, bubbles, and convulsions that ramified through society, and they have eroded long-standing social bonds that gave stability and meaning to many lives. Markets, rather than religion or government or family or ideology, seem to be the most dynamic and powerful force in our world.

Markets today raise hard questions about what it means to lead responsibly. What is responsible leadership when leaders confront so much uncertainty, when their jobs and their organizations seem temporary and fragile, when performance pressures focus everyone on short-term metrics, and when leaders don't have enough control of people and activities to deliver on longer-term commitments? Do leaders' responsibilities shrink as they understand and control less and less of what lies ahead? For leaders and organizations in intensely competitive circumstances, the ready guide to responsibility and ethics may not be basic human values, the wisdom of respected executives, or the principles of moral philosophy, but the world-weary observation of the German playwright and poet Bertolt Brecht: "First food, then ethics."[3]

This book examines the challenges of a market-driven world from an unusual perspective—with struggle as a central idea—and offers practical guidance for meeting these challenges. Struggle has always been part of leadership, but typically in the familiar sense that leadership is often hard, risky work. This book is different because it takes a much closer look at struggle. It argues that leaders now face certain critical, recurring struggles and that struggling well is critical to leading responsibly and successfully in our world of exciting, dangerous, intensely competitive, always-on markets.

The challenge today is even more difficult because the rapid pace of change in many markets does more than create really hard problems for leaders. It also makes solutions harder to find, because it weakens the familiar institutions and guideposts that have guided leaders in recent decades. Boards of directors, traditional regulation, statements of corporate values, classic debates about accountability to stakeholders and shareholders, and even familiar ethical principles have become less relevant and useful. This creates especially hard challenges for men and women who take their responsibilities as leaders seriously.

Lessons from Entrepreneurs

This book describes these challenges in detail, explains why we face them, shows why they are here to stay, and offers practical guidance for men and women who want to lead successfully and responsibly under these conditions. The book does this, in part, by drawing on the experiences and reflections of entrepreneurs. They are, in effect, guides who have already explored the intensely competitive, often uncertain, and sometimes deeply unstable world that many other managers have been entering. One of the founders of FedEx said that the early years were like "taking a supertanker at full speed over a reef with a quarter of an inch to spare."[4] In addition, a world that is complex, fluid, exciting, and dangerous requires broad, flexible, imaginative thinking, so this book also draws upon a wide range of case studies, research findings, provocative analogies, and contrarian ideas, as well as longstanding philosophical perspectives on life and work.

What emerges from this perspective is a striking view of responsible leadership. It says that men and women seek positions of leadership and take their responsibilities seriously—despite the struggles involved and even *because* of them. These men and women are seeking "the good struggle." This is a cause or a challenge that demands and merits their best efforts, really tests their competence and their characters, and helps them lead lives they deeply value. They may well fail to make good on their commitments and aspirations, because a market-driven world offers few guarantees, but the good struggle is worth the risk and cost.

This book argues, in essence, that responsible leadership is, quite often, a version of the good struggle: it is a long effort, demanding perseverance and courage, to make good on serious but profoundly fallible commitments in an uncertain and often unforgiving world.

Notice the critical elements in this definition. One is struggle, and the others are commitment and courage. We basically understand what these three words mean, but they have now taken on more complex and important meanings, and this book offers an explanation of why they are especially important for understanding responsible leadership today and knowing how to lead other people, successfully and responsibly.

This is not a dramatically new view of leadership. Though it is sometimes portrayed as an exciting adventure, leadership has always been an uphill effort demanding strength of character, deep resolve, tenacity, and a measure of faith—in one's self, in others, and in some larger aim or cause or mission. However, in a world of intense, global, technology-enhanced, always-on markets, the hill is steeper, simple survival can be a hard challenge, success is often fleeting, the pressure to play games or fixate on short-term metrics grows stronger, and leadership demands even more tenacity, confidence, grit, and faith. Struggle has always been central to accomplishing anything worthwhile, and this is especially true today.

Markets Everywhere

I reached these conclusions in the middle of a research project that started with an entirely different focus. My original aim was learning what, if anything, was different about responsible leadership in small, new companies. The rationale for the project was that most of our thinking about responsible business leadership is based on large, stable, well-established firms.

For decades, for example, the paradigm case of responsible leadership has been Johnson & Johnson's handling of the Tylenol crisis. This is the story of how the company and its CEO, James Burke, responded to the deaths of seven people who took Tylenol contaminated with cyanide in 1982. When this happened, Johnson & Johnson was a century old, had sales of $6 billion, annual profits of $500 million, a diversified range of businesses, strong brands, and many products that dominated their markets. Most of its leaders had worked together for years. In contrast, the typical entrepreneurial company is new, small, short on cash, has no reputation or brand, no ongoing relationships with regulators, virtually no staff, and faces intense competition from other new companies and, quite often, well-established, powerful firms. Its management team is often newly formed and fluid.

What I soon realized, however, is that, in some very important ways, the entrepreneur's world is becoming almost everyone's world. Even the largest, most entrenched, and comfortable companies now face intensifying market pressures to innovate, and do so rapidly and continuously. In their benign form, these pressures say innovate and prosper; the malevolent version says innovate or die. I soon realized that the entrepreneurs I was studying were not a special subgroup of leaders. They were living and working in a world that many others were now entering. These others are leaders—of teams, departments, units, and entire organizations—in both the private and public sectors.

As a result, I shifted my focus from responsible leadership in smaller companies to responsible leadership in a market-driven world. This world has two defining features: powerful, ubiquitous markets and ceaseless recombination. Both elements are fundamental, and each intensifies the other.

There are now markets for almost everything—companies, components, funds, capabilities, government influence, brilliant human talent, cruel child labor, and even bodily organs. Many markets are global and operate around the clock. Many are intensely competitive. What happens in these markets is the extraordinary phenomenon of almost continuous recombination. Ideas, parts of organizations, technologies, funds, and people now move ceaselessly—sometimes rapidly, sometimes efficiently, sometimes convulsively—among organizations.

As they do so, they are reshaped and evolve in new, often surprising directions. The original computer mouse, developed by Xerox and costing $16,000, became an easy-to-manufacture, $15 device after Steve Jobs had taken and "improvement engineered" the idea. And because people, technologies, and entire units of organizations are sold and resold in markets, many organizations are almost continuously shifting their shapes. Some survive, some prosper, and many struggle and fail, even after prospering for a period. But the surviving pieces—valuable ideas, talent, technology, and residual funds—do not evaporate.

They are bought and sold and then recombined in other products, services, and organizations.

Two commanding social thinkers, who disagreed on so much, foresaw this market-driven world. One was Karl Marx and the other Joseph Schumpeter. Marx died in 1883, the year Schumpeter was born. Marx, of course, condemned capitalism and forecasted its collapse. Schumpeter was a strong advocate of capitalism and believed that entrepreneurship was its engine. Nevertheless, their foundational ideas, viewed jointly, provide a powerful insight into economies and societies today.

Marx believed market-driven capitalism would oppress the proletariat by driving down their wages. The reality now is that market-driven capitalism is pressing hard on everyone, except the most privileged or protected. Schumpeter famously defined entrepreneurship as "recombination." Today, powerful markets around the world are driving creative and often disruptive recombinations of funds, technologies, people, and ideas—at a pace even Schumpeter might find astonishing.[5] Dynamic, exciting, relentless, fascinating, seductive, dangerous, and sometimes convulsive markets surround, suffuse, and shape a good deal of our work and our lives.

To be clear, I am not arguing that the impact of markets that many people are experiencing today is unprecedented. In capitalist economies, organizations and their leaders are often pressed hard by competitive pressures, technology can lead to dramatic changes in markets and society, and depressions can rock entire economies. The argument here is that, for a variety of reasons, market pressures in recent years have become more widespread, more intense, and have affected more levels of organizations than they did in the postwar decades, when competition in many important industries was primarily national and oligopolistic rather than global, manufacturing-based rather than knowledge-based, and involved incremental rather than rapid, disruptive change. It is these recent developments that, I believe, call for a rethinking of responsible leadership.

Beyond the Industrial Statesman

A recombinant world with intense competitive pressure takes a familiar model of responsible leadership, the product of the institutional and ideological landscape of the last century, and renders it incomplete, misleading, and sometimes hazardous. The exemplars of the classic model were, until recently, known around the world: Thomas Watson, Jr., of IBM, Konosuke Matsushita of Panasonic, Alfred Sloan of General Motors, James Burke of Johnson & Johnson, and a handful of others. These names are fading, but their legacy remains in the form of a powerful, distinctive way of thinking about responsible leadership.

These men—and they were virtually all men—were industrial statesmen. They led giant companies, sometimes for decades, and found ways to earn extraordinary returns for shareholders. At the same time, the industrial statesmen created good jobs for employees and worked closely with a fairly stable group of stakeholders. Their companies were huge, highly integrated operations, run by hierarchies of managers, and were typically focused on manufacturing. These firms were stunningly productive, created unprecedented wealth, and amassed extraordinary power—over competitors, industries, communities, and even governments.

Because some giant firms abused their power, governments created systems of governance to hold the firms and their leaders accountable. The exemplary industrial statesmen met their responsibilities within these systems and used their power responsibly. They also promoted corporate values that shaped the work and even the lives of their employees, an undertaking facilitated by long-term or lifetime employment. All this made for a powerful conception of responsible leadership.

Now the world that created the industrial statesman is receding. We need a view of responsible leadership for a world in which managers are pressured to innovate continuously and dramatically; find themselves in fluid, uncertain, and intensely competitive environments; and run companies enmeshed in temporary, sometimes unstable, partnerships and networks that often span national boundaries and many cultures. Their organizations look less like giant, quasi-permanent, twentieth-century hierarchies and more like fluid, permeable networks that compete—like many entrepreneurial firms—by rapidly and successfully assembling and reassembling resources of all kinds. This institutional setting is very different from the one that shaped the model firms of the twentieth century and their leaders.

This makes the question of responsible leadership in a market-driven world urgent and challenging. In fact, a natural temptation is to ignore the question on the grounds that the whole idea of responsible leadership is naïve. In a remorselessly competitive world, doesn't a company have to play the same game everyone else is playing? How much responsibility can an individual afford in a world in which very few jobs are secure? In a turbulent and uncertain world, can we really hold anyone responsible for very much when they may actually control very little? And in a world with many cultures and varying ethical practices, can responsible leadership really mean much of anything?

One way to avoid these questions about markets and responsibility is by going up to the top of the mountain, far above what Shakespeare called the "hurly-burly" of everyday life, and saying that capitalism has always been turbulent and that the basics of responsible leadership have always been the same. In other words, this era and its challenges are nothing special.

To a degree, this approach is sound. Capitalism has never been placid or predictable, and the fundamentals of responsible leadership seem to be timeless. That is, responsible leaders take their legal and ethical obligations seriously, they work with others to make good on the basic obligations of their organizations, and they often make and keep broader commitments to stakeholder groups, communities, and societies. All this is simple, clear, and fundamentally true.

But history, institutions, and culture matter. A Roman centurion leading his men into battle, a Chinese mandarin directing a government bureau, a tribal elder confronting a drought, and the CEO running General Motors when it was the most powerful company on earth all faced very different challenges and worked in very different cultures and institutions. This is why, if we want to understand responsible leadership today, we have to look in depth and detail at how, for better and worse, markets now shape the context in which leaders work and live.

To study responsible leadership today, I relied on two strategies. One was empirical and the other conceptual. The empirical strategy is described in the appendix. In essence, it involved reading scores of case studies and books about entrepreneurs, interviewing entrepreneurs, and interviewing many of my colleagues in the Entrepreneurial Management Unit at Harvard Business School, who have decades of experience studying entrepreneurs and working with start-up companies as founders, directors, and investors. I also looked closely at the experiences of leaders in larger organizations who faced high levels of turbulence and uncertainty because of crises in their organization or shocks outside them.

The conceptual approach was going back to basics— and doing it in an unorthodox way. I drew heavily on my years of studying the responsibilities of leaders and of teaching students and executives about these responsibilities and developed a set of questions that define, I believe, the core of responsible leadership. My claim about these questions is a strong one: the questions can be phrased in different ways, but they are enduring questions. In other words, for responsible leaders, these questions are inescapable, they come with the territory, and responsible leadership consists of thoughtful, lived answers to them.

Because these questions are so important, this book is organized around them. Each chapter focuses on one of the enduring questions of responsible leadership and explains why it is fundamental to responsible leadership. Then each chapter presents the answer to the question that evolved during the last century, explains why these familiar approaches are no longer adequate, and sketches the answers that are emerging today.

The chapters paint with broad strokes. There were, of course, no "twentieth-century answers" to the enduring questions. In this book, "the twentieth century" is shorthand for a particular phase of capitalism that began with the rise of large industrial firms in the late 1800s and continues today. And entrepreneurs existed throughout the last century, though many more have flourished in recent decades as countries, particularly the United States, developed infrastructures to create and support new businesses.[6] In short, the "old" world of giant firms and industrial statesmen has not disappeared, and it overlaps with the "new" market-driven era, just as one geological age overlaps with the next.

The Enduring Questions

The first enduring question asks, *Am I really grappling with the fundamentals?* We associate responsible leadership with sound values and effective action, but the first responsibility of leaders is actually intellectual and analytical. This question asks if leaders have thought hard about the forces shaping the economy and the society around them and the full implications of these driving forces. Managers who don't meet this responsibility can easily lead their organizations in the wrong direction or lead them badly, even if they have sterling characters and are deeply committed to all the right values. When they fail to meet this first responsibility today, markets move swiftly and remorselessly. The price of failure can then be damaging to the livelihoods, hopes, and lives of hundreds or thousands of other people.

The second question is, *Do I know what I am really accountable for?* This is an enduring question for two strong reasons. One is managerial and practical: leaders need to know what their basic job is, what they are responsible for accomplishing, and what counts as success and failure. The other reason is societal: without clarity about accountability, society cannot guide and control how leaders use their power; leaders then drift, and they can revert to serving their own interests.

The third enduring question asks, *How do I make critical decisions?* All men and women who have had real responsibility can recall situations, often in vivid, sometimes wrenching detail, in which they had to make long-term, high-stakes decisions for their organization in conditions of uncertainty, with the risk of failure looming large. Critical decisions are acute tests of responsible leadership.

The fourth question asks, *Do we have the right core values?* Today, almost every organization has some sort of values statement. These are often broad, vague, and inconsequential. But this enduring question asks about core values. It suggests that leaders put aside mission statements and lofty words and instead assess their real values—the ones that a leader and an organization will struggle hard and long to make good on when the chips are down and sacrifice is unavoidable. Organizations always have core values in this sense—they may be explicit or implicit, managed or serendipitous, admirable or deplorable—but responsible leaders work hard to create the right ones.

The final enduring question is also about values, but with a personal focus. It asks, *Why have I chosen this life?* From a distance, positions of leadership are alluring: they offer status, power, pay, and the opportunity to make a difference in the world. But, close up and day by day, leadership can be a tough, wearying task. Leadership has always been hard work, but its challenges are even greater now because more organizations face higher degrees of uncertainty, complexity, and market turbulence. And these pressures are felt by leaders throughout organizations, not just at the top. So the final enduring question asks leaders to think hard about the issues to which Dag Hammarskjöld devoted his periods of quiet reflection and journal keeping: Is this struggle worth it? What is it doing to my life and for my life?

Emerging Answers

Are there answers to the enduring questions that reflect the challenges and opportunities of leading today? No one has a crystal ball, but a new guiding perspective seems to be emerging, and the experience of entrepreneurs brings it into focus. The best way to understand this view of responsible leadership is by looking carefully at what may be the emerging answers to the enduring questions. The rest of this book presents these answers in detail, but their basic elements can be summarized briefly.

The first enduring question asks leaders if they are grappling with the fundamentals. The fundamentals today are ubiquitous, intense market pressures and continuous recombination. As a result, the central task for responsible leaders today is not doing the right thing or serving shareholders or stakeholders. The first task of responsible leaders today is intellectual. It is a ceaseless, demanding effort—involving close observation, imagination, data gathering, and analysis—to understand the swirling context around organizations today and set a sound direction. Failure at this task is often punished swiftly, and organizations and many people then suffer serious hardship.

The second enduring question asks about the accountability of leaders. The emerging answer is that our familiar institutions of accountability—boards of directors, law and regulation, and government oversight—are becoming much less effective because of the pace and complexity of market-driven change. These institutions, designed for another era, all too often lag behind the activities of innovative leaders and the rapid movements of sophisticated, often global markets. The result is extraordinary and disconcerting: to a significant degree, leaders are left to define their own accountability. This places a great deal of responsibility in leaders' hands. It takes confidence, determination, and courage to accept that responsibility and then, through commitments, to take personal responsibility for achieving certain aims for certain groups and resisting pressure from others.

The third enduring question asks how leaders should make critical decisions. The emerging answer is that, in a recombinant world, responsible leaders can often do little more than make open-ended, evolving, and fundamentally fallible commitments. These are fleshed out, in time, through experiment, experience, error, failure, and serendipity—and, above all, a willingness to struggle long and sometimes courageously to learn, adapt, and eventually move roughly forward.

When leaders today look for a serious answer to the fourth enduring question—What are our core values?—they need the courage to move beyond what has become the consensus approach and instead think and act for themselves. The consensus approach consists of lengthy lists of commitments to universal principles such as honesty, integrity, respect for individuals, and so forth. What matters today are core values—defined by what an organization and its leaders are willing to struggle for when the chips are down and real sacrifices have to be made. And, in a market-driven world, these core values have to take markets seriously. They have to sometimes accelerate, sometimes transcend, and sometimes block the market forces around organizations.

Finally, when responsible leaders ask the last enduring question—Why should I take on the burdens of leadership?—they have to think about commitment and struggle in very personal ways. The reason to take on the rigorous challenges of leadership today has to be more than compensation, status, or the allure of success, because talented people can achieve these in other ways, typically by becoming specialists of some kind in banking, consulting, technology, or a traditional profession.

At a deeper level, men and women sometimes choose leadership because of what its challenges and struggles mean to them. This is because responsible leadership is a good struggle. It is a long, rigorous challenge that tests their competence and their characters fully, gives purpose and intensity to their lives, and helps them lead the kind of lives they really value. They may not make good on all their commitments and aspirations, and their careers may evolve in ways that surprise, disappoint, or even derail them—because a recombinant world offers few guarantees and markets are indifferent to the fates of individuals—but the good struggle nevertheless seems worth the risk and cost.

It is easy to romanticize the notion of a good struggle, but this struggle demands an unusual trait of character, best described as managerial courage. It is easy to think that we understand courage, and it usually seems simple. We think of powerful, familiar examples, such as the physical courage of a firefighter rushing into a burning building to save someone or the moral courage of protestors fighting tyranny. Courage seems to be doing the right thing out of dedication to some principle or ideal and despite personal cost or danger.

For responsible leaders, however, courage looks somewhat different. It is, in essence, the courage of the long slog, not the single moment of bravery. It is the strength—intellectual, moral, emotional, and even physical—to make sound but fallible commitments for oneself and an organization, and the strength to struggle hard and creatively hard to make good on these commitments. It is the courage to endure and persist through long periods of vulnerability. It involves a willingness to take risks, to sacrifice, and to doggedly pursue some larger, higher aim.

Managerial courage doesn't involve looking danger or death in the face, but it does involve hard, sustained, ambitious work in the pursuit of something worthwhile—despite uncertainty, risk, doubt, and almost inevitable frustrations and roadblocks. Managerial courage isn't the valor of the *Iliad*, in which we see brave men fighting hand to hand on the plains of Troy, but the resolute tenacity of the *Odyssey*, the story of Odysseus bringing his men home on an arduous, decade-long voyage.

The Broader Contexts

It is important to keep the struggles of leaders in a global perspective. For hundreds of millions of people today, work and life are a harsh struggle against disease, poverty, oppression, and despair, and this has been the lot of humankind for most of history. Millions of others, in developed countries, struggle daily to support themselves and their families on minimal wages. Against this background, the "struggles" of leaders today—that is, the workplace difficulties of people who are paid well, enjoy power and status, and live in comfortable homes with clean water and safe, nourishing food at their fingertips—don't rank among the world's urgent problems.

The struggles of leaders today also need historical context. From this perspective, the challenges are nothing fundamentally new. Leadership has always demanded commitment, struggle, and courage, and leaders today may simply be experiencing afresh the tumultuous world of classic Anglo-American capitalism. Its turbulence was tamed, temporarily and partially, particularly in the postwar decades of the last century, in industries dominated by large, oligopolistic firms. During this era, responsible leadership was defined, to a large degree, by stable institutions and clearly defined structures of roles and responsibilities. What is happening now may simply be a return to the open-field, brawling capitalism that preceded the rise of giant, powerful industrial companies—with the added complexities of global competition, instant communication through digital networks, and network-style organizations.

But historical or global perspectives provide little consolation for leaders who live and work in the vortex of market-driven recombination. They face a distinctive set of demanding challenges, uncertainties, and pressures. Their organizations and the livelihoods of many people depend on whether they meet these challenges. And even successful leaders can have a strong sense that, despite hard work and long hours, they might not be up to the responsibilities and demands of their positions.

A market-driven economy can be extraordinarily dynamic and exciting. It can be a cornucopia of ideas, jobs, progress, and wealth, but it also confronts leaders and managers with a grueling combination of intense performance pressure, uncertainty, and complexity. This is why it is very important to find contemporary answers to the enduring questions of responsible leadership.

CHAPTER TWO

AM I REALLY GRAPPLING WITH THE FUNDAMENTALS?

Many children, all around the world, play a game called "Chutes and Ladders" or "Snakes and Ladders" that is actually an ancient Indian game. This simple, innocent amusement serves as a remarkably accurate and disconcerting image of life and work. In the game, players roll dice and try to move from the bottom to the top of a decorated board. Landing on a ladder lets a player move rapidly toward the top and victory, and landing on a chute or snake means sliding downward. In just a few moves, players can move rapidly up to the brink of success, and then lose almost everything on the next move.

Although the game is now a pastime, the original Indian version had a serious moral purpose. It taught children that the way to live good and useful lives—in an uncertain, volatile world—was by developing particular traits of character. The snakes on the board were surrounded by symbols of lust, anger, murder, and theft, and the ladders by symbols of generosity, faith, and humility. In today's chutes-and-ladders world, character matters enormously for responsible leadership, and the critical, defining traits of character are the courage to make fundamentally fallible commitments and to struggle, persistently and sometimes courageously, to make good on them.

The ladders around us are exciting, sometimes stunning innovations in a wide range of fields. Sir Arthur Clarke, the British science fiction writer and inventor, once wrote, "Any sufficiently advanced technology is indistinguishable from magic."[1] His description fits what is now happening in consumer electronics, telecommunications, medicine, genetic engineering, and many other fields. These developments are part of a worldwide wave of market-driven innovation and entrepreneurship, whose range and force were captured in the title of a recent book, *Billions of Entrepreneurs*.[2]

The chutes and snakes today are instability, uncertainty, and turbulent markets. Less and less now seems stable, predictable, or safe. In recent years, huge companies, such as Citibank and GM, have nearly collapsed. Firms with longstanding commitments to quality and safety, such as Toyota and BP, suffered calamitous problems. Of the twenty-five "most powerful" people in US business in 2003, seventeen were no longer on the list just four years later.[3] In 1960, it took two decades for the *Fortune* 500 to change a third of its companies; now it takes four years.[4] Entire economies now operate on a chutes-and-ladders basis: for example, between 1985 and 2010, the US economy experienced several major economic crises, each worse than its predecessor. To protect themselves against whatever may come next, American firms have accumulated historically unprecedented cash balances of nearly two trillion dollars.[5]

While markets are rational to a degree, they are also deeply human institutions. Their complexity reflects the imagination and ingenuity of the human mind but also our hopes and fears. As a result, bubbles, crashes, collusion, chicanery, herd instincts, emotional blindness, puffery, and shocks are also familiar aspects of market behavior—as the last decade has made so clear. Financial markets, which are probably the closest approximations of what economists call perfect or complete markets, are riddled with human vulnerabilities.

Behavioral economics has been documenting these for nearly two decades and has basically confirmed Warren Buffett's observation that "wild things happen in the markets. And the markets have not gotten more rational over the years . . . when people panic, when fear takes over, or when greed takes over, people react just as irrationally as they have in the past."[6]

What is going on? What forces are creating this exciting but perilous world? And what does it mean for responsible leadership? To answer these questions, leaders need to address the first enduring question and ask themselves: Am I really grappling with the fundamentals?

Intellectual Responsibilities

This question may seem like an odd starting point for thinking about responsible leadership. The question doesn't ask about ethics, values, or corporate social responsibility. It doesn't ask about decision making or action, which typically define leadership. But leaders will fail to deliver on their responsibilities if they haven't thought deeply about the full implications, for themselves and their organizations, of the powerful forces shaping the economies and societies around them.

This is why the first responsibility of leaders is intellectual. It is the struggle to develop—to the extent possible—a deep, careful, analytical, data-driven understanding of the driving forces in the markets and society around them and to keep this understanding loose, flexible, and revisable. This approach is different from both the meticulous planning of the great industrial companies of the last century, which was well suited to a stable world whose evolution they often shaped, and from the often romanticized, passionate opportunism often associated with entrepreneurs.

In recent decades, managers have become much more sophisticated in thinking about one set of fundamentals, the economic and competitive forces that drive competition in their industries. Economists, consultants, and other analysts have developed elaborate tools for analyzing the basic economics of firms and industries. Skeptics criticize these techniques, saying that jargon, pseudoquantitative models, and high consulting fees mask basic ideas that every successful merchant has understood since the beginning of commerce.[7] But even the skeptics recognize the importance of actually grasping the fundamentals, and Warren Buffett put the reason succinctly. "When a management with a reputation for brilliance," he wrote, "tackles a business with a reputation for bad economics, it is the reputation of the business that usually remains intact."[8]

The search for the fundamentals is hardly confined to business strategy and actually reflects an age-old view of leadership and life. Shakespeare expressed it in *Julius Caesar,* where he wrote:

> *There is a tide in the affairs of men*
> *Which, taken at the flood, leads on to fortune;*
> *Omitted, all the voyage of their life*
> *Is bound in shallows and in miseries.*[9]

Shakespeare's view is a very broad one, and the first enduring question takes this perspective. It asks leaders to do more than analyze the competitive forces currently shaping their industries. The first enduring question asks about the deeper and more powerful driving forces that shape entire economies and societies and asks leaders to grapple with what these deeper forces mean for their organizations.

This effort won't produce final answers, but is well worth the time and energy. Sometimes the effort produces valuable insights. It can help leaders escape the crucial but hazardously narrow focus on today's agenda, the quarter's numbers, competitor tactics, and organization politics. Trying hard to grasp the fundamentals can also reduce the chance of being blindsided, by encouraging the mental habit of looking for emerging patterns and odd developments with larger implications. It also promotes modesty, a healthy, low-level paranoia, and vigilance rather than hubris. In the end, most decisions are bets on the future, and by struggling for clarity about the fundamentals, leaders improve their odds.

But the most important reason for responsible leaders to grapple with the fundamentals today is that a new set of fundamentals may be emerging—with profound implications for how they should make decisions, structure their organizations, commit resources, and even live their lives. In this book, the shorthand for these new fundamentals is "a market-driven world" and "the new invisible hand."

The best way to begin understanding the implications of this emerging world is somewhat surprising. It involves looking away from the world around us and taking a historical perspective. By looking briefly at the fundamentals that shaped society, organizations, and business economics in the recent past, we can see the new fundamentals in sharper relief. We also begin to see why thinking in terms of *fallible* commitments, as well as perseverance and courage, is especially important for understanding leadership today.

The Era of Big Machines

For the leaders of organizations, the fundamentals that shaped the last century were scale, hierarchy, and control, and their power is reflected in what they created: giant, quasi-permanent companies that dominated the social and economic landscape and provided stable jobs for their employees and significant, stable benefits for other stakeholders. These firms appeared in every industrial country, and their names are familiar: GM, IBM, Sony, Philips, Daimler-Benz, Deutsche Bank, and Shell.

After millennia in which a business was just a tiny, one-person operation—a hatmaker, blacksmith, or apothecary—these huge firms, and many others like them, appeared on the scene. Where did these giant organizations come from? To radically simplify a very complex story, the Industrial Revolution replaced muscle power, from humans and animals, with mechanical power from the steam engine. Then came a long series of mechanical, engineering, and scientific breakthroughs— through the efforts of amateurs and tinkerers and then scientists and engineers—that enhanced and exploited the new sources of energy. And then bold entrepreneurs and financiers saw and seized opportunities to create larger and larger manufacturing operations that took advantage of these developments. These large-scale plants were basically huge machines that cranked out ever larger and faster flows of products.

But these giant plants created a serious practical challenge for the leaders who created and ran them. How could leaders control these operations and ensure efficiency, quality, and profits? And how could they accomplish this as their operations expanded? The answer was a brilliant managerial breakthrough: controlling these operations through hierarchies of salaried managers. No single person could understand, much less manage, these giant organizations, but the new hierarchies of managers could. They broke down the immense challenge of controlling the new industrial operations into separate tasks, assigned managers responsibility for these tasks, and then had other, higher-ranking managers monitor and coordinate everything.

This achievement was chronicled by the renowned business historian Alfred Chandler in *The Visible Hand*.[10] Chandler's title brilliantly encapsulates his central idea: the visible hand of management replaced Adam Smith's invisible hand of the market in wide swaths of the modern economy. Managers in meetings decided where resources would go, not buyers and sellers in markets. Raw materials went in one end of giant industrial machines, products came out the other, and hierarchies of managers controlled what happened in between. Often, these managers also tried to control the markets for raw materials that went into their giant organizational machines, through vertical integration and long-term contracts.

They tried to control the markets in which they sold their products, through cartels, price fixing, and other arrangements. Their overriding aim was controlling and accelerating the flow of production and profits.

In short, for much of the twentieth century, big was beautiful, powerful, and stable. High-volume manufacturing reduced the cost of manufactured goods dramatically. The giant hierarchies developed and controlled critical technology and, when they could, did the same with market forces. The ultimate result was companies and industries that, for the most part, changed incrementally. And this reflected a broader trend in society, one that Max Weber, the renowned sociologist, called "bureaucratic rationality"—the imposing of control systems and logical rules on previously organic or unruly spheres of human activity.[11]

When business leaders understood, either explicitly or intuitively, the fundamentals of scale, hierarchy, and control and took advantage of them, they typically achieved profits, stability, and sometimes dominance. We know the names of their companies, because so many of them—such as Coca-Cola, IBM, Panasonic, and BMW—remain powerful and successful today. Other firms, which failed to develop economies of scale and scope, languished and often collapsed. Almost no one today has heard of the Hudson Motor Company or Magnusson Computer Systems.

When the new industrial giants abused their power, they were criticized, vilified, and regulated. When they seemed to be contributing to society, they were praised as models of the future because they provided advanced technology, good jobs, tax revenues, profits, and high-quality products at ever-declining costs. Their leaders—the industrial statesmen—were heralded and became role models of responsible corporate behavior.[12] This was because they understood the fundamentals of their era. They secured profits and power by leading hierarchies of managers in their firms, developing and implementing mass-production technology, and using this power to shape and sometimes dominate the markets around them.

The New Fundamentals

Now these same two forces—markets and technology—are weakening and sometimes destroying the giant machines. Instead of taming technology and markets, longstanding hierarchies have sometimes become their playthings. Many of the giant firms of the last century have recently faced severe challenges, and some have teetered near bankruptcy. The reason for this dramatic change is a new set of fundamentals.

The fundamentals today can be summarized simply: we are living in Joseph Schumpeter's universe, surrounded by the ever-accelerating, market-driven recombination of resources—what he called the "perennial gale of creative destruction." Put abstractly, more and more of our economic and social life is being divided into modules. These modules are now bought and sold and recombined in ever more powerful, sophisticated, and sometimes dangerous markets. This recombinant world—a world of modules moving in markets—is full of extraordinary opportunity, complexity, fragility, and uncertainty.

What has happened? The answer is that the invisible hand of the market has reemerged in an extraordinarily powerful, sophisticated form. In fact, a central challenge for economic historians today is describing and explaining what is distinctive about contemporary markets and organizations. The tentative consensus among business historians is that capitalism today, which is sometimes called "entrepreneurial capitalism," has some features of the small-scale "personal capitalism" that Adam Smith described and other features of the "managerial capitalism" that Chandler conceptualized, as well as important new characteristics.[13]

Everything Is a Module

There are many important forces shaping economies and societies today. The familiar list includes environmental challenges, the crowding of the planet, inequality and poverty, the Internet, and globalization. But another fundamental force is particularly important for understanding responsible leadership today because it is so powerful and pervasive and has serious implications for men and women who want to lead responsibly.

The simplest way to describe this force is somewhat abstract. In essence, much of our economic and social life, and more and more products and activities, are being divided into modules. These modules are now bought, sold, combined, and recombined in ever more sophisticated and fast-moving markets.[14] This is a tectonic change from a world of aggregation, control, hierarchy, and efficiency—exemplified by the giant industrial machines—to a world of unbundling, modularization, networks, and markets. These are the new fundamentals, and responsible leaders need to grapple with their implications. The best way to understand this new world is by looking at its basic elements, which are modules and markets.

What is a module? The abstract answer is that a module is a component of some kind that can be combined with other components in a system. The everyday, real-world answer is that almost everything around us is a module or consists of modules. Inside every car or computer is a multinational coalition of complicated modules, some assembled from complex submodules. Entrepreneurial companies are literally assembled from capital, talent, and ideas, and most reconfigure themselves several times in their early years. Even giant companies are behaving similarly: over the last ten years, GE has bought more than $88 billion in high-tech assets and sold more than $55 billion worth.[15] The managing partner of a major private equity firm recently surveyed this scene and observed, "Everything is assembly now."[16]

Society has been evolving in similar ways, unbundling a wide range of traditional activities into small units and selling them in markets. In many two-earner families, the work of the traditional housewife has been modularized by outsourcing child care, cleaning, shopping, and other tasks.[17] Political candidates and pollsters no longer focus on large demographic groups, such as conservative males, and instead microtarget small subgroups and try to assemble them into winning coalitions. People once had a single career with one organization; now careers are modularized as individuals move among employers.[18] And millions of people have abandoned long-established religions, taking elements from various traditions and creating their own personal, recombinant faiths—a practice sometimes called "cafeteria religion."[19]

Looking even more broadly, we see a world, once organized around bipolar superpowers, the United States and the Soviet Union, that has devolved into shifting coalitions of countries. At the same time, a number of countries have been fragmenting into loose assemblages of regions and tribes. And we find terrorist organizations and global criminal groups that consist of quasi-independent cells that coalesce temporarily around specific operations.[20]

The forces driving these changes run strong and deep. They seem to be seizing a good deal of our familiar world, breaking it into pieces, and then rearranging it or leaving things scrambled. Princeton historian Daniel Rogers has written that we live in an "age of fracture."[21] His phrase captures a widespread sense, shared by analysts from many disciplines, that profound shifts are now under way and affecting almost every aspect of life and society.[22]

The final evidence of the modularization of almost everything is the widespread concern about the phenomenon and the deep issues of ethics and responsibility it raises. The mortgage-backed securities at the center of the recent financial crisis were highly complex recombinations of individual mortgages whose cash flows were sliced into tranches and sold separately. Some entrepreneurial companies that cost investors millions of dollars were "built to flip" (i.e., rapidly assembled for quick profits), not built to last. Will "cafeteria religion" provide the wisdom, guidance, and solace of faiths that have stood the test of time? Should genes, the building blocks of life, be patented and sold like other industrial commodities? And the debate about outsourcing stirs real fears in developed countries and even in some emerging ones—about lost jobs and, at another level, about the possibility that human beings are just complex soft-tissue modules cast hither and yon by unrestrained market forces.

Many factors are contributing to what seems to be the modularization of almost everything, and markets are among the most powerful forces driving this change. Basically, they are encouraging people and organizations to create more modules, to combine them in a widening range of ways, and to do so rapidly, creatively, and aggressively. The visible hand of management may have replaced or suppressed markets during the era of the giant industrial machines, but now the invisible hand of the market has reasserted itself—in an all-pervasive, extraordinarily powerful, exciting, volatile, and corrosive form that is penetrating and shaping almost every sphere of work and life.

This fundamental feature of the new invisible hand creates particular challenges for leaders. A recombinant world is fragile, which makes long-term commitments less reliable and credible. It intensifies competitive pressures and makes a short-term focus even more compelling because a clever reassembler can copy today's innovation tomorrow. As a result, the mantra "innovate or die" can become "innovate and still die." Recombination also makes it much harder for leaders to inculcate values when people in their organizations know they and their leaders are basically modules in a plug-and-play world and could be moving on soon. The natural instinct in these circumstances is to take care of yourself, here and now, and follow Bertolt Brecht's adage about bread before ethics.

The New Invisible Hand

It is easy to praise markets. During the last two decades, more than a billion people have been lifted out of grinding poverty as markets and capitalism spread to China, India, and other countries. It is also easy to condemn markets. The global economic crisis spread like a deadly contagion through world financial markets and then to "Main Street" markets, nearly causing a worldwide depression. The overt lesson is that markets are powerful, valuable, and perilous.

The subtler lesson is that markets have become stunningly complex and interconnected. Markets are not the simple, one-time, price-driven transactions between buyers and sellers described in basic economics textbooks. They are social creations that now take an endless variety of forms and serve a vast array of human purposes. In recent decades, markets have evolved, proliferated, adapted, and specialized, and they are continuing to do so, at an ever more rapid pace. Adam Smith would likely be astonished at today's incarnation of the invisible hand.

This development has altered the fundamentals for responsible leaders. Their central task is no longer the efficient operation of a large, wholly owned, manufacturing firm focused on national markets and a handful of stable stakeholders. The emerging challenge is entrepreneurial: creatively assembling and reassembling resources in once familiar markets that have grown very complex, and in altogether new markets. The best way to see this is by looking briefly at familiar markets and seeing how complex and sophisticated they have become. Many of the individual elements in this picture are familiar, but their cumulative impact is remarkable.

Customers. The market for customers is probably as old as the human race, and protohumans may have had versions of it. Usually, we think of this market in simple, familiar terms, such as grocery stores and car dealers, but it has become as complex and challenging, strategically and psychologically, as any human activity.

The competitors in many industries today include large global firms, start-ups, alliances, competitors linked in networks, and governments. In some businesses, competing for customers requires multiyear efforts by teams of sales reps and engineers with PhDs. And technology can rearrange the playing board at any time: new developments, arising anywhere in the world, can change customer dynamics everywhere. If we view competitive strategy in the contemporary markets for customers as a game, it can make many online multiplayer games look like child's play.

More and more markets today work like economics textbooks say they should. Customers have ample choices, many just a call or a click away. Margins are under pressures, profits get competed down toward zero, and leaders have little margin for error. Ethics can become, in effect, 2 percent. If companies spend too much pursuing responsibility, their prices go up and customers vanish. If they cut corners and play games, customers find out and move on. The pressure never goes away.

Funds. Like the market for customers, financial markets have also grown vastly more complex and fluid, creating a stunning range of opportunities and threats. The "old-fashioned" financial markets of the twentieth century relied on stock markets and banks. After the Depression-driven reforms of the 1930s, financial life became simple and stable. Commercial banks made loans to individuals and companies, and investment banks issued stocks and bonds for large companies. Banks were caricatured as boring: the

"3-6-3 rule" said that successful bankers borrowed money at 3 percent, lent it at 6 percent, and played golf at 3 p.m. For the most part, credit flowed cautiously.

Now, banks are among the most complex organizations in the world, they operate around the clock, "financial engineers" design their products, and the large banks are barely comprehensible to outsiders and, in some ways, to their regulators and even their own senior executives. And banks are now only one element of financial markets. During the last decade, for example, the so-called shadow banking system emerged. This is a multitrillion-dollar global network of commercial banks, investment banks, hedge funds, and providers of credit default swaps—all closely and complexly interconnected.

Talent. The third familiar market, the market for talent of all kinds, has also grown far more complicated and competitive. The classic twentieth-century firms provided lifetime employment, or at least long-term employment, for outstanding employees—which took these employees out of the labor market. The companies tried to recruit the best and the brightest, trained them—often for many years—and inculcated their values. Loyalty was a central company value: companies took care of their own, in return for dedication, flexibility about assignments, and willingness to relocate.

Now corporate loyalty is waning all around the world, as more companies view layoffs as standard practice. The other reason is the rise of an always-on, sophisticated market for talent. Even in the current weak economy, the market for many kinds of talent remains robust.[23] Talented individuals have become free agents, akin to professional athletes and actors. They are temporarily loyal to their current employers and permanently loyal to their careers.[24]

The market for talent reflects the recombinant economy and also accelerates it—by creating an ever-larger pool of individuals with complex, multicompany backgrounds. A successful entrepreneur recently observed that Silicon Valley employees felt embarrassed if they had worked at a company for four or five years, because the best people get frequent offers to work elsewhere and sooner or later take one. At the same time, companies now take advantage of complex labor markets with much more sophisticated approaches to hiring. In the "old days" of quasi-lifetime employment, they hired for basic skills and ability and then relied on training and acculturation to produce the managers they needed. Now, companies often search for "plug-and-play" talent that can immediately make specific contributions.

Information. The market for information is longstanding, but not as familiar as the markets for customers, funds, and talent. For millennia, rival organizations—Athenian city-states, medieval kingdoms, Persian satraps, Phoenician merchants, warring armies, and commercial traders—have sought to gain advantage by garnering intelligence, inside perspectives, and even the tiniest wisps of information. Today, the same interests and dynamics play out on a global scale with incomprehensibly large amounts of information about virtually everything. And because this information often has value, markets of all kinds develop to buy and sell it, such as websites that track the movements of corporate jets, which can supposedly help bankers assess the probabilities of mergers and acquisitions by seeing where executives spend time.[25]

Capabilities. In the last two decades, a new perspective on corporate strategy has shown how much companies compete on capabilities—the ability to make something better, quicker, or cheaper than competitors—as well as on products and services. The critical capability today is the ability to innovate and produce a stream of competitive products at competitive costs. Today, few leaders believe their organizations can do this on their own, so they compete aggressively for partnerships to secure crucial capabilities.

This is a major change from the twentieth-century model of the firm as more or less a fortress that tried to develop and own all the capabilities it required. This meant having its own production and marketing operations, minimizing dependence on suppliers, and doing almost all R&D in-house. Now the autarkic model is the exception, not the rule. The reason is a longstanding cliché: the "knowledge explosion." No company, no matter how large, can now develop and control all the knowledge, skills, technology, and relationships it needs to compete successfully. For example, roughly half of all new drugs are produced by partnerships of various kinds.[26]

Hence, firms compete hard for capabilities and do so through a stunning array of new organizational arrangements. Many firms, including very large, wealthy companies such as IBM and Procter & Gamble, with billion-dollar R&D budgets, rely on "ecosystems" of partnerships for important capabilities. These let firms move in and out of markets quickly, experiment with new approaches, meet the increasingly varied and demanding requirements of customers, and block competing firms from access to partners. And the partnerships and networks mutate quickly. Today's important supplier can become tomorrow's minority equity investment or joint venture partner.

Government Influence. Since ancient times, businesses have sought strategic government support to shape the rules of the game in their markets and raise their chances of success. A founding executive of Halliburton, the oil field services company, made this point with breathtaking clarity when he said, "The right politician at the right time can make you very rich."[27] Companies competed with other firms, and often with labor unions, interest groups, political parties and others, to shape law and regulation in helpful ways. The competition was never easy—because it was often a high-stakes, zero-sum contest against determined adversaries, such as national labor unions—but it was much simpler than today.

If twentieth-century competition to influence government policy and shape markets was checkers, the new game is chess, and almost all firms, even small ones, have to compete by its intricate rules. In the twentieth century, only multinational firms needed complex, multicountry government strategies. Now, because many small firms and many new ones are competing in global markets for customers, funds, talent, information, and capabilities, and because, for well and ill, government policy shapes markets in so many ways, almost all firms are vigilant and active in the market for government influence.[28]

Meaning. This is an odd-sounding, little-noticed market, but it is perhaps the most powerful and disconcerting evidence of how pervasive markets have become. Human beings seem to have a built-in "explanatory drive"—we want to make sense of what is happening around us.[29] In traditional societies, religion and rulers, along with tradition, gave people a sense of order and meaning. In modern societies, people supposedly get more information in a day than medieval peasants did in a lifetime, but we deal with this bombardment in the age-old way—by searching for patterns, trends, and meaning.

But we don't do this alone. A wide variety of institutions compete hard to provide sense and meaning for us.[30] To accomplish this, many organizations now rely on sophisticated media strategies designed to imbue their goods, services, and activities with value. Companies work hard to make their products and services meaningful for customers; social activists do it to advance their causes; politicians vie to tell us why their agendas really matter to each of us personally; and religions increasingly compete, through marketing and media, to fill pews.

If an organization's activities and leadership are viewed positively, it is much more likely to succeed in all the other markets in which it competes directly. In addition, it is more likely to be successful in the market for government influence. A clear example is the recent Toyota recalls. Before they occurred, Toyota stood for safety and reliability. But the recalls created problems in every one of the markets in which Toyota competed and put it under severe scrutiny by government regulators in several countries. As a result, Toyota has spent several years recovering from a disaster in the market for meaning and its impact on the other markets surrounding the company.

Faced with multidirectional competition and continuous recombination, how can leaders tell if they are really grappling with the fundamentals and doing it in the right way for their organizations? The answer, put succinctly, is that when leaders are really grappling with the fundamentals, a particular intellectual trait becomes central.

Intellectual Honesty

Arthur Rock, a renowned and extraordinarily successful venture capitalist, is essentially a world-class expert on leadership in turbulent, complex, high-stakes situations.

His career in Silicon Valley began in 1971 and has spanned four decades. Rock was an early investor in Intel, Fairchild Semiconductor, Apple, and many other important firms. The leaders and companies he worked with confronted the new invisible hand in its most exciting and unforgiving form. Typically, they were trying to create and ride waves of profound technological change. They faced intense market pressure because many other firms were crowding into the same areas, and these companies, in their early years, were highly recombinant, with mobile talent, technology, funds, and customers.

In the latter years of his career, Rock reflected on what made for a promising investment in this type of company. He didn't say analytical skill, breakthrough technology, or a great business plan. Instead, he pointed to a trait of character. What really mattered, Rock said, was intellectual honesty.

For someone seeking astute investment advice, this answer can seem like small potatoes. Everyone is in favor of honesty—for entrepreneurs, other leaders, and the rest of humanity. But Rock and his partners didn't help create some of the most important companies in Silicon Valley and earn hundreds of millions of dollars by endorsing the platitude that honesty is the best policy. For Rock, intellectual honesty meant something quite different, subtler, and more challenging.

Rock defined intellectual honesty with a deceptively simple question. When entrepreneurs sought his backing, he asked himself, "Do they see things the way they are, and not the way they want them to be?"[31] The crucial word in this definition is "see." Rock was looking for men and women who would struggle hard and successfully for clarity—about what they knew and didn't know, about what they could and could not control, and about the real risks and opportunities in front of them.

Intellectual honesty tests a leader's mind. It requires intellectual capacity, in-depth knowledge about a product and an industry, an acute sensitivity to customers, an eye for emerging patterns, and a willingness to rethink assumptions as complex interactions create surprising new situations and issues. But this intellectual work is only one part of the challenge facing responsible leaders when they grapple with the fundamentals today. The other part is psychological and emotional. It tests the heart and character of leaders.

Fallibility

If leaders were androids, intellectual honesty would be relatively simple. They could just follow the facts and analysis wherever they led. And, when this didn't produce clarity and answers, robotic leaders would create decision trees, assign probabilities to possible outcomes, and choose the one with the best expected value. In reality, however, a commitment to intellectual honesty often leads to hard struggles because its intellectual challenges are commingled with psychological and emotional ones.

Actual flesh-and-blood leaders are, in Friedrich Nietzsche's phrase, "Human, all too human."[32] The new invisible hand surrounding them is a vast, churning, and significantly unanalyzable kaleidoscope of activities, opportunities, and threats. This makes the pursuit of intellectual honesty a long, often frustrating endeavor. It often produces little more than a partial, transient sense of shifting, opaque scenarios.

Intellectual honesty often reveals uncomfortable facts, bad trends, or disappointing or threatening possibilities. It often means facing serious risks and problems. This is hard for many leaders. They are typically men and women with abundant confidence, optimism, and strong faith in themselves, their work, and the people around them. They also know that negative sentiments from a leader can spread like a contagion. So when so much of the future is blank space, the strong temptation is to look away from the prospect of failure, hope things improve on their own, and fill their imaginations and the company airwaves with upbeat statements.

The challenge of intellectual honesty is even harder because periods of elation and overconfidence can alternate with pessimism. Jeff Bussgang is a general partner at Flybridge Capital Partners, which specializes in early-stage investments, and has served as a director at more than a dozen start-up companies. He offered this perspective: "Sometimes you think you're building a billion-dollar company and sometimes you're certain you're going to run out of cash and have to lay off the team and shut it down."[33] These negative feelings are compounded by weariness, because turbulence, the effort to decipher complexity, and performance pressure all take a physical and mental toll.

In addition, a sense of personal responsibility makes entrepreneurs feel that everything rests on their shoulders and that they have little margin for error. As the founder of several small companies put it, "You have the ball. You're responsible and accountable and everybody is looking to you to make something happen. And there's usually no safety net."[34]

Running through these thoughts and feelings is powerful tension. On one side is an intensely personal commitment to an enterprise and faith in its possibilities. On the other side is a sharp, at times painful awareness that so much long, hard, costly effort could well result in utter failure. This tension is entirely realistic. In an entrepreneurial world, the strongest, best-planned commitments are inevitably fragile.

At a deeper level, the struggle to see things as they are reminds leaders of the fundamental fallibility of their endeavors and the need to live and work with the continued vulnerability this entails. Professor William Sahlman of Harvard Business School, who has studied and worked with entrepreneurs for three decades, warns them about "the big eraser in the sky" that can come down at any moment and "wipe out all their cleverness and effort."[35]

Entrepreneurs and many other leaders now live and work in a world of fallible commitments, and this can create real obstacles to grappling, successfully and responsibly, with the fundamentals. In a world of fallible commitments, it takes courage—in the precise sense in which Aristotle defined it—for a leader to grapple with the fundamentals. For Aristotle, courage was a midpoint between the extremes of recklessness and timidity—and entrepreneurs' fears can drive them toward one extreme. Confidence, hope, bedrock optimism, and elation can drive them toward the other.

An old saying tells us, "We see the world not as it is, but as we are." The challenge for leaders in a market-driven world—and it is often a profound challenge—is grappling with the fundamentals not simply as analysts or thinking machines, but as full human beings. In other words, grappling with the fundamentals means grappling with oneself. As one longtime observer of entrepreneurs put it, "Many of the biggest problems for entrepreneurs are inside their heads."[36]

Intellectual Ambition

Intellectual honesty can sound daunting and often leads to struggles for leaders, but it can also be an exciting undertaking for leaders who are intellectually curious and ambitious. Today, leaders of organizations have front-row seats at the extraordinary social, economic, and technological changes unfolding in the world all around us. Huge companies, such as the old IBM, are rising and falling and sometimes rising again. Entrepreneurs are combining new and old technologies and activities to produce a stunning range of new products and services.

Oliver Wendell Holmes, Jr., an important American jurist and philosopher, once said, "It is required of a man that he should share the passion and action of his time."[37] Holmes felt strongly that this was serious business. The risk of not doing this was the terrible possibility, as he put it, "of not having lived." A commitment to clarity about what really matters for an organization, what is really changing in the world around it, and what opportunities of creative recombination lie at hand is a demanding, exciting, rewarding, and crucial task for responsible leaders, in just the way Holmes described.

Gabrielle Chanel, who became known as "Coco" after she developed a line of women's clothing that expressed a distinctive and contemporary style, began her career as a hatmaker in Paris early in the last century. Chanel had an acute eye for trends in fashion. She also understood that the invention and spread of the sewing machine was creating new manufacturing opportunities. At the same time, extraordinary new retailing outlets—the large department stores that relied on the advanced technology of electrical lighting—were exciting and attracting thousands of new customers. Chanel understood these opportunities intuitively, and not through market or industry analysis. Her intense engagement with trends in fashion and her understanding of new ways to make and sell hats created the foundation for what became an extraordinary entrepreneurial success, particularly for a woman in the early part of the last century.

Grappling with the fundamentals isn't simply reading analysts' reports. It often involves active search and investigation of opportunities, the best of which, almost by definition, are in unexplored or underexplored territory or in fields undergoing rapid change. In recent years, for example, large firms have been racing to develop opportunities in China, but some entrepreneurs began doing business there decades ago. They had all the advantages and risks of first movers, and their leaders had front-row seats for watching and, in small ways, participating in the extraordinary economic transformation of China.

In short, if a version of "Snakes and Ladders" were created for leaders in an entrepreneurial world, one of the most conspicuous symbols on the board would represent the courage of intellectual honesty and ambition in the face of uncertainty, volatile emotions, and exciting but uncharted opportunity. It would somehow represent both the analytical and personal challenges of grappling with the fundamentals and the value of struggling hard and courageously to see the world as it is. But comparisons to the ancient Indian game take us only so far. In that game, everyone can look at the board and see the hazards and opportunities. In contrast, in a recombinant world, leaders have to create their own ladders, and they often know little or nothing about the location of the dangerous chutes.

They can only succeed if they are intensely committed—despite the vulnerability and fallibility of these commitments. Although the rest of this book focuses on the other enduring questions, the emerging answers to all of them strongly reflect the basic answer to the first enduring question. The almost inescapable context for responsible leadership today consists of powerful, sophisticated, recombinant, and sometimes harsh and volatile markets. This is an exciting world because it prizes innovations and innovators, but it is also a dangerous and challenging environment for men and women who want to lead successfully and responsibly.

Their everyday world is heavily defined not just by opportunity, but also by intense performance pressure, burgeoning complexity, rising uncertainty and risk, and fragile, fluid organizations. It is a world of profoundly fallible commitments, and intellectual honesty about this world and its full implications for an organization is the first, essential, and inescapable step toward responsible, successful leadership.

The next two chapters take a closer look at what these fallible commitments mean for leading responsibly. One chapter asks, If commitments are harder and harder to make in an entrepreneurial world, then what am I really accountable for? The next asks, How do I make critical decisions in a responsible way, when I can foresee and control so little?

CHAPTER THREE

WHAT AM I REALLY ACCOUNTABLE FOR?

The ancient Romans posed a question that all societies answer in one way or another. Their question was, "Quis custodies ipsos custodies?" or "Who guards the guardians?" The guardians are individuals and groups with power over other people, and the Romans understood, from hard experience, why these people needed oversight. Otherwise, they would use their power to serve their own interests and not society's. A fundamental challenge for any society is holding its guardians—business executives, government officials, doctors, police officers, and others—accountable for how they use their power.

At the same time, the guardians themselves need standards of accountability, and so do their organizations. Leaders need to know what their basic responsibilities and tasks are, what counts as success and failure, and how they will be judged and rewarded. Without clarity about accountability, leaders and their organization can drift or zigzag aimlessly. Hence, for leaders, the second enduring question is, What am I really accountable for?

During the last century, industrial societies evolved a brilliant way of holding business leaders accountable. This solution defined clear roles and responsibilities within a larger set of institutions. It said, in effect, these are the groups whose interests you must serve, these are your responsibilities to them, and these are the groups that will monitor and reward your performance.

Now, with market forces surging, this classic approach is weakening. Its replacement is a new, surprising, even disturbing system of market-based accountability. If we ask who guards the guardians today, the answer is that, to a significant degree, they guard themselves. Their accountability is heavily defined by the commitments they choose to make in the markets and communities surrounding their organizations. To understand how radical the emerging system of accountability is—and why struggle, commitment, and courage play central roles in it—we will start by briefly examining the system of accountability it is replacing.

Vertical Accountability: Boring and Brilliant

During the twentieth century, the rise of huge, powerful corporations raised extremely difficult issues of accountability. These firms appeared in every advanced economy, and their economic and political power threatened many other groups in society. At one point, GM had sales larger than the gross domestic products of all but four countries and had operations in every US Congressional district. Hence, one of the great issues of twentieth-century society was controlling giant companies and getting them to serve society's interests. In time, a solution emerged: societies took hierarchical management, which was critical to running the industrial giants, and used it to control the giants.

The symbol of hierarchy is a table of organization—which unfortunately makes hierarchy seem simple, familiar, bureaucratic, and dull. But hierarchy is a brilliant social invention. It enables mere human beings, with all their limitations and foibles, to coordinate complicated activities on a vast scale. The Romans relied on hierarchies of military officers and administrators to conquer and rule a vast empire. Two millennia later, sophisticated hierarchies enabled business leaders to control huge organizations despite their technological, economic, logistical, and human complexity.

The brilliance of hierarchy is its fusion of knowledge, power, and responsibility. Hierarchies take large-scale, complicated activities and break them down into small spheres. Then individuals with the right knowledge and skills are put in charge of each sphere. They have clear tasks and duties. A boss assesses their performance, and higher-ranking bosses hold this boss accountable. Hierarchy is basically vertical accountability. Front-line employees are responsible to supervisors, supervisors to managers, managers to vice presidents or other senior executives, and these executives to the CEO.

Vertical accountability was society's solution to the problem of giant, powerful companies. The CEO was given a boss, the board of directors. The board was accountable to shareholders or other stakeholders, regulatory agencies supervised the companies, legislatures created laws and regulations, and society held legislatures accountable through democratic elections.

Reality, of course, was much messier, but the idea of accountability through hierarchy had extraordinary conceptual and practical power, and it pervaded twentieth-century society. Churches led by bishops, armed forces headed by generals, and towns headed by mayors were all variations on the same basic theme. Vertical accountability became the secular counterpart of the medieval "great chain of being," in which God presided over an orderly universe through ranks of angels, kings, local rulers, and family heads.[1]

Vertical accountability is easy to criticize, and it can degenerate into inward-looking, mind-numbing bureaucracy. But this system of accountability co-evolved with the economic miracle of the twentieth century and helped lift billions of people from cruel, dirt-floor poverty. Technology, markets, and secure property rights also played critical roles, but vertical accountability controlled, focused, and legitimated the historically unprecedented economic and political power of the giant industrial machines of the twentieth century and the guardians who ran them.

Vertical accountability remains important today, but it is now weakening, conceptually and practically, because of the new invisible hand. It is eroding the brilliant fusion of knowledge, power, and responsibility. The problem emerged in the last decades of the twentieth century and has grown acute in recent years.

The Vacuity of Vertical Accountability

For business leaders, the conceptual problem with vertical accountability is lack of an answer to the fundamental question of whether CEOs and boards are accountable for earning returns for shareholders or for serving the interests of a wider range of stakeholders. This question sparked a heated debate that spanned almost the entire twentieth century. The controversy was valuable because it raised important issues of political and economic philosophy, but the debate never ended and its central question remained unanswered.[2]

CEOs and boards handled this problem, mainly by finessing it. They focused primarily on profits but also heralded their firms' broader contributions to society—and the industrial statesmen showed the way. With their "industrial" hats on, they ran companies focused on profits, growth, and returns. As statesmen, they persuasively explained their firms' contributions to stakeholders—in the form of jobs, technology, tax revenue, and financial support for community activities—and thereby legitimated their firms' power and profits. Market power often made this approach both possible and prudent. For example, IBM CEO Thomas Watson Jr. was once asked why his company could afford to be so progressive, and he supposedly replied, "It's because my daddy didn't start a meat packing company."

In recent decades, however, the chronic problem of shareholder-versus-stakeholder accountability became acute. One reason was Japanese and then Asian competition. This led to outsourcing and layoffs, which drove a large wedge between the interests of owners and those of workers and local communities. Another was hostile takeovers, which hammered the wedge in further. And a third factor—swift-moving, recombinant markets—changed the accountability debate in a more profound way, by draining away much of its meaning.

Consider the side of the debate that says CEOs and companies are primarily or exclusively accountable to shareholders. Who are these shareholders? Are they sophisticated institutions with a long-term perspective, individuals managing their retirement accounts, senior executives with stock-based compensation, sovereign wealth funds representing the interests of other countries, computer programs tracking indices, traders who hold shares for a few days or hours, or supercomputers doing high-frequency trading and moving in and out of stock in nanoseconds? The ownership of most publicly traded firms now turns over rapidly. So are CEOs accountable to today's mix of owners or tomorrow's or to some imagined mix of both? The relatively stable institutional and individual shareholders of the last century have been replaced by a continuously recombining array of owners.

The stakeholder accountability view has a similar problem. During the last century, a company's stakeholders were often fairly clear—a stable group of employees, their union, the local community, local and federal government, and a fairly stable group of shareholders. But who are "the stakeholders" for a global firm? These companies have hundreds of significant groups with stakes in what they do, and the group changes as the firm's strategy and the economy change.

By the end of the last century, the two sides of the accountability debate resembled a pair of exhausted boxers propping each other up after a long prizefight. Each side still had avid fans, but the basic logic of vertical accountability remained unresolved. There was no answer to the central question of corporate purpose: To whom were executives and directors ultimately accountable and what were they accountable for? This was a very serious problem with vertical accountability, but it wasn't the most serious.

The Impotence of Vertical Accountability

Critics of academia sometimes refer to an imaginary professor who says condescendingly, "That may be true in practice, but let's see if it's true in theory." The crucial problem with vertical accountability is that it is now failing in practice as well as theory. By the end of the last century, boards of directors and government regulators—two critical rungs on the ladder of accountability—were widely criticized and often failing conspicuously. The most vivid evidence for this conclusion is the calamitous pair of bookends—the Enron scandal and the global financial crisis—that began and ended the last decade.

The Enron collapse was appalling in its own right, but it was only one of many firms, large and small, that collapsed with the Internet bubble. By every standard of traditional accountability, Enron had a first-rate board, as did many of the other firms that collapsed, and Enron and these other companies were regulated by a wide range of state and federal bodies. What went wrong with these boards? Their members were distinguished, successful leaders, but they typically did too little, too late. Yet, with hindsight, their failure seems almost inevitable.

How could part-time outsiders, however well-intentioned and successful in their own lines of work, assure accountability for complicated firms competing in a wide range of businesses around the world and engaged in rapidly evolving, highly complex activities? Most boards meet about six times a year, spend two days on each meeting, and now devote a substantial and increasing portion of this time to issues of process and compliance. This leaves little time for getting below the surface of complex issues.

The interests and ingenuity of CEOs often compounded this problem. How can a board of part-time outsiders avoid being dominated by full-time insiders with the skills, information, relationships, and savvy to run large, complex organizations? This question almost answers itself. And some CEOs have serious reservations—expressed only in confidence—about the real value of all the time and energy boards require. The head of a large and very successful private investment firm put the point bluntly, saying that the absence of a conventional board meant he could concentrate on the three groups that really mattered to a business: customers, investors, and employees.[3]

Even CEOs who try to develop collaborative relationships with their boards sometimes have these reservations. A highly respected former CEO, currently a director of several prestigious firms, said recently that as long as boards failed to get executive compensation under control, it was hard to take the rest of their governance efforts seriously.[4] Unfortunately, large-scale statistical studies confirm that boards have often failed to link executive compensation to company performance. Instead, executive pay is driven by some mix of managerial power and larger market forces.[5]

After Enron and other firms failed, the US Congress passed the Sarbanes-Oxley reforms. These were designed to strengthen board governance. But how well did they work? The answer involves the other calamitous bookend of the last decade: the financial crisis that nearly caused a worldwide depression. The Sarbanes-Oxley regulations may have achieved unseen victories, but they didn't conceal or repair the deep flaws of traditional vertical governance. All of the banks that collapsed or teetered near the brink had impressive boards of directors, typically made up of hard-working, thoughtful, highly experienced and successful executives. Because of the Sarbanes-Oxley reforms, their audit committees consisted primarily of independent directors with financial expertise, yet very few boards and firms avoided the massive financial train wreck.

Many factors contributed to this failure of vertical governance, but market-driven recombination played a central role. The financial products and services offered by large banks are extremely complex and are traded daily in massive volumes in swift-moving markets. The financial crisis revealed that many experienced traders, their managers, and firm CEOs did not grasp the full complexity and implications of the products they were buying and selling and the interconnected markets surrounding their firms. If insiders were significantly in the dark, how much can be expected from part-time outsiders, the members of boards of directors?[6]

And all this happened while the other crucial element of vertical governance, government supervision, also failed—even in giant commercial banks, such as Citigroup, that have been closely regulated for decades by a multitude of government agencies. With hindsight, we can see important gaps in bank regulation, but why did they exist? One factor is the difficulty regulators face keeping up with myriad, complex innovations in multi-trillion-dollar markets for financial services. Another is the influence Wall Street firms have on the US Congress and regulators, which typically discourages regulation and other limits on CEO or corporate power. But Wall Street is hardly alone in these efforts. Corporations of all kinds are active in the market for government influence, and even the smallest changes in vertical accountability—such as fuller disclosure of the details of executive compensation—can meet implacable resistance.[7]

In short, the balance of power has been tilting toward CEOs and insiders and against boards of directors and government regulators. This seriously weakens vertical accountability. And, in all likelihood, market-driven recombination will further strengthen the power of executives. If any party can comprehend what is happening inside recombinant companies and rapidly changing global markets, it is the CEOs and senior managers of these firms. They are immersed for sixty or seventy hours a week in the complexities of their organizations. They have knowledge, relationships, and control over information. And they typically achieved their positions of leadership through talent, unremitting hard work, savvy, and street smarts. All these resources can be deployed to limit or impede the other parties involved in traditional governance.

New Century Financial Corporation, a fast-growing, and then bankrupt mortgage company, is a clear and dismaying example. The company, founded in 1995, grew rapidly. Its strategy depended heavily on originating subprime mortgages and then creating collateralized debt obligations (CDOs) from them or selling the mortgages to banks that did so. After the housing market weakened in 2005, warning signs flashed for New Century. During an eighteen-month period, its board of directors met twenty-two times and the audit committee of the board met sixty times; despite these efforts, New Century went bankrupt. Time and litigation may eventually show how much corruption, negligence, or CEO dominance contributed to this and other catastrophes. But its products were innovative, complex, and hard to understand and value, which made it even harder for outside parties, and apparently New Century's own board of directors, to evaluate the company's operations and risks.

The challenge for society and its political institutions is enormous, comparable to the one created more than a century ago by the rise of the giant industrial machines. Their executives were powerful because their control of these huge, highly profitable operations gave them economic and political clout. Today, the power of executives originates in knowledge—about the complexities of technology, the pace of recombination, and the vast range of opportunities created by global markets—and their power is likely to grow as the global innovation race accelerates. Innovation often outruns, sometimes by long stretches, entire bodies of existing regulations, laws, and norms of ethical behavior.

Moreover, many of the innovations today involve complex combinations and recombinations of complex modules, and the only people who fully understand the complexities are the leaders and the teams directly involved with them. This was true of CDOs, the Toyota braking systems, and the BP operations a mile under the Gulf of Mexico. These parties' assessments of risk, benefits, opportunity, and hazard mattered critically. Other groups were on the outside looking in and often arrived much too late: regulators ended up practicing emergency room medicine after a calamity had occurred, instead of providing preventive care.

In short, vertical accountability has suffered a double blow. It is failing conceptually because it lacks an ultimate standard of accountability. It is also failing institutionally, as boards and regulators struggle to keep up with the ever-accelerating complexity and the pace of change in and around the organizations they are supposed to monitor. Even worse, some boards and regulators are often strongly influenced by the leaders they are supposed to oversee. So where does this leave us? Who guards these powerful guardians?

Horizontal, Market-Based Accountability

A new system of accountability is displacing the old one. It is governance by markets and not by traditional institutions such as boards and regulatory bodies. It is "horizontal" in the sense that markets, as explained in the last chapter, surround and even permeate companies today. And it is multimarket accountability because it relies on all the markets surrounding firms—not just financial markets, but the markets for talent, partners, ideas, customers, and meaning—to direct and constrain leaders and firms. The essence of the emerging system of accountability is that leaders and organizations make commitments in markets—more precisely, sharply defined, codesigned, evolving, and sometimes dramatically shifting commitments—and these commitments are enforced by the powerful markets that surround many companies.

The basics of the emerging system are simple. Leaders and companies make commitments in markets. If a company succeeds, markets make more resources available and give companies and their leaders more discretion. If a company fails, markets withdraw resources and put their leaders on shorter leashes. New ventures are a clear example. They grow and prosper in small steps, each of which attracts or fails to attract funds, talent, ideas, and other resources from surrounding markets. And when new ventures fail, these markets withdraw resources, often swiftly. This same combination of discipline and opportunity is now reshaping large companies, even global giants, as their leaders lose the ability to control and suppress markets and must now succeed or fail in the multiple markets surrounding their firms.

Horizontal accountability is becoming more common for reasons we have already seen: markets of all kinds are growing more powerful and more sophisticated, which makes it harder for companies to use the market-impeding tactics that many twentieth-century leaders relied on. These included self-financing of major investments to reduce pressure from the market for funds, locking in customers through a wide range of practices, integrating backward and playing quasi-dependent suppliers against each other, relying on lifetime employment to limit the market for talent, creating huge, autarkic, in-house R&D labs to minimize dependence on external ideas and capabilities, vigorously lobbying all levels of government to limit competition, and relying on their leaders to serve as public statesmen and build broad support for a company.

Many executives still use these tactics when they can, but a Schumpeterian world makes this harder to do. More and more companies are now disciplined by markets of highly specialized investors, customers, potential and actual strategic partners, and restless, talented individuals. Markets give these groups options. So, when a company fails to serve them, they can and do move on. These markets are particularly powerful because they often reinforce each other: when customers move on, investors, talented employers, and partner firms often follow them in pursuit of better opportunities.

This development is striking, attractive, and disturbing. The emerging system is striking because its operations and its implicit ethics are so different from classic vertical accountability. That system gave leaders defined roles and specific responsibilities in a larger, fixed structure of monitoring, assessment, rewards, and penalties. This system has hardly disappeared—leaders are still bound by laws, regulations, reporting relationships, and fiduciary duties—but a recombinant world seriously weakens the brilliant fusion of power and responsibility of vertical accountability. For well and ill, markets now guard the guardians.

As a result, the question of a leader's accountability in an entrepreneurial world has a distinctive ethical answer. The question is not simply, What are my duties in the framework of rules and requirements defined by a classic vertical hierarchy of bosses and regulatory oversight? The question is also, What commitments have I made and what commitments have we made as an organization to individuals and groups in the markets and societies around us? Viewed this way, the commitments that define accountability in an entrepreneurial world are creative moral acts. They do not involve subordination to some established rule of society or a decision made by a boss. Instead, accountability originates in an obligation to make good on the spirit of some jointly designed, provisional, and evolving objectives.

Horizontal, multimarket accountability is attractive, at least in principle, because it seems so well suited to a fluid, recombinant world. One reason is that markets are so powerful and intrusive. They may be the only social institution with the power and sophistication to hold firms and their leaders strictly accountable. Lateral accountability doesn't rely on vague pseudometrics such as shareholder value or stakeholder benefits. Instead, it holds companies and their executives responsible for achieving a series of specific objectives. If business leaders make good on these commitments, their companies survive and prosper. If not, they have to renew their efforts, renegotiate their commitments, or face failure.

Accountability through market commitments is also attractive because it combines this powerful, external discipline with a good deal of flexibility. The best way to see this is by looking at how entrepreneurs create businesses. When entrepreneurs start out, they have a wide range of choices. They can search far and wide for partners and resources. In time, they eventually create a customized set of commitments. They work out detailed financial commitments for a particular group of investors, commit to providing and developing a particular kind of product or service for a particular subset of customers, make employment commitments to the talent this effort requires, and often set up partnerships to secure capabilities they need. They may also make broader social commitments to the communities and societies around them.

The advantages of market-based accountability—powerful, vigilant, external monitoring, and flexibility and adaptability in a fluid world—can easily be obscured by caricaturing it as wild-West, greed-driven, anything-goes capitalism. In contrast, the reality is that well-functioning markets require active and independent governments that can enforce the law, assure a minimal but critical level of business ethics, remedy externalities, and promote fair and open competition. This is a fundamental and profound truth about successful capitalist economies and both vertical and horizontal accountability.

A similar misconception involves corporate social responsibility in a world of horizontal, market-driven accountability. The caricature is that companies and their leaders have to follow the dictates of markets and have scant time or energy for broader social initiatives. But this answer ignores the crucial role of creativity, freedom, and commitment in a market-based world. Leaders and their organizations are free to pursue a wide range of efforts— as long as they can assemble a coalition of other parties, in markets and communities, who will provide sustained support.

Many entrepreneurial firms make strong commitments to social responsibility and do so with the full support of the investors, employees, partners, and other groups in the markets surrounding them. In many cases, these social commitments help entrepreneurial organizations attract the talent, partners, and investors they need. Other entrepreneurial organizations go even further and create hybrid recombinations of what were traditionally viewed as for-profit and not-for-profit organizations.

One example is Generation Investment Management, which was created in 2004 to focus on investments involving long-term sustainability. The firm made its objectives clear, hired analysts with a distinctive set of values and backgrounds, and succeeded in raising several billion dollars in investment funds and earning strong returns.[8] Another is the Aravind Eye Hospital in Madurai, India—a large-scale, high-efficiency, almost industrial operation— whose founder had asked himself, "Tell me, can cataract surgery be marketed like hamburgers? We have to do something like that to clear the backlog of 20 million blind eyes in India."[9]

Some analysts now argue that a new economic sector is emerging, based on what has been called the "for-benefit enterprise." These are creatively recombinant organizations, as a recent overview of these efforts made clear: "For-profit businesses are tackling social and environmental issues, non-profits are developing sustainable business models, and governments are forging market-based approaches to service delivery. Out of this blurring of traditional boundaries, a different model of enterprise is emerging, driven by entrepreneurs who are motivated by social aims."[10] Over the last two decades, social entrepreneurs have arguably changed the landscape of education, development, public health, and poverty relief around the world.[11]

Nevertheless, the performance pressures of a market-driven world can be acute. This means that, in most cases, leaders need to find social commitments that reinforce their overall strategies and help them create and sustain important relationships in the markets, ecosystems, and societies around their organizations. The margin for error is simply smaller in an intensely competitive world. As a result, leaders need to think carefully and analytically, not passionately and inspirationally, about how the social commitments they make will affect their organizations and the complex markets around them.

IBM's response to the horrific South Asian tsunami in 2004 is a dramatic example of these possibilities. Hundreds of IBM employees responded within hours of hearing the first news. Within days, the company had created a new database that enabled local people as well as relief officials to record and learn about casualties, illness, logistics problems, and other needs. Soon after, the company created telecommunication systems linking emergency personnel across the region. And, once the immediate crisis was over, IBM began working with the United Nations, the United States Agency for International Development (USAID), and other agencies to share the technology it had developed and enhance their preparedness for the next disaster.

This was an exemplary corporate social responsibility project. It had a clear focus, built on IBM's strengths, drew in other organizations with complementary resources, and helped meet a serious social need.[12] In all likelihood, IBM employees gained new skills, the company built or strengthened relationships with other parties in its ecosystem, and it might have developed technology it could market in the future. IBM's leaders and employees could feel genuine pride in how quickly and aggressively they helped address a massive social problem.

The combination of flexibility, customization, and demanding accountability all make horizontal accountability seem—in principle, at least—quite attractive. But it is also disturbing. This approach leaves a great deal to markets, and markets often fail. Powerful market actors can make demands that serve their interests rather than an organization's—something that founders sometimes accuse venture capitalists of doing. Moreover, there is no assurance that government will take steps to assure that markets will remain healthy and serve larger interests. Government may act too late, as it did in the financial crisis, or it may be unduly influenced by the interests of powerful firms.

Yet for all its hazards and challenges, market-based accountability is here to stay, at least for the foreseeable future. As a result, leaders who want to manage responsibly face especially demanding challenges when they ask the second enduring question—What am I really accountable for?—and try to make good on sharply focused but evolving sets of personal and organizational commitments.

Market-Based Accountability and the Good Struggle

Lateral accountability can sound attractive, even exciting. Leaders can, in principle, survey the world and then decide what commitments they want to make to which groups. They are their own guardians, because they can initiate and shape the specific commitments they make in the markets and communities surrounding their organizations. But lateral accountability also explains why struggle and courage define responsible leadership today. There are four reasons for this.

First, market-based accountability imposes stringent demands on leaders. Once they make a commitment, leaders typically have to meet clear, demanding performance targets and do this under close scrutiny. Investors, customers, critical employees, technology partners, communities, and others parties don't say, "Great idea. Take our time and resources and support, good luck, and keep us posted." Instead, they often create a series of interim targets and carefully monitor how well or poorly a leader is meeting them.

Second, external parties often want a role in important decisions and bargain hard to get it. Markets empower these parties—because a world of markets is a world of options. Investors, talent, strategic partners, and other market and community groups with resources critical to a particular organization usually have alternatives, so they can bargain hard for significant roles in decisions. They want to influence, step by step and stage by stage, how their resources are being used, the risks they are running, and the share of the pie they get.

Venture capital and private equity firms are clear examples of this. They have no interest in funding financially autonomous baronies. They invest in stages and work with entrepreneurs to create short- and medium-term benchmarks for performance, and partners from these firms work closely with the executives of portfolio companies to provide guidance and expertise of all kinds. These investors have the power to protect their interests by actively monitoring and sometimes intervening, and they use it.

Venture capital firms are typical of many the parties involved with entrepreneurial companies. They know that these organizations are assemblies of funding, talent, capabilities, and initial customers. In the short run, various parties may be closely tied to a new company. So, during this period, they want a strong hand in decisions. And they get this role because, in the medium run, they can exit. Just as venture capital firms can deny or reduce their next staged investment, the best talent can move the fastest to other opportunities, strategic partners can reduce the resources they provide, and customers can go elsewhere.

The third reason why lateral accountability creates difficult struggles for leaders is that leaders have to meet these challenges while they are managing ever more complex organizations. Twentieth-century organizations have been described as islands of management control surrounded by a sea of market relationships. But now markets are swamping the islands. Information, people, and funds flow continuously across the boundaries of organizations, in response to market forces.

If the classic image of the twentieth-century firm was an assembly line or the giant River Rouge complex built by Henry Ford—a vast machine that took in iron ore and rubber and cranked out Model Ts, under the control of a hierarchy of career Ford executives and managers—the new image is the firm as a platform. Organizations, particularly entrepreneurial ones, are increasingly platforms for a wide range of ever-shifting, module-like activities.

The challenge now is that more and more organizations are complex hybrids of the old and the new. Hierarchy has not disappeared. Companies are still organized into large, stable organizational blocks, and these operations need to be stable, focused, and efficient machines. But extraordinary complexity arises when traditional hierarchies must exist under the same organizational roofs as fluid, ever-shifting networks of market-driven modules. If an organization today isn't highly focused and efficient, competition will eat away its margins and it will fail. At the same time, if an organization isn't a nexus of information, knowledge, learning, experimentation, and ingenuity, it will ossify and die.

If the old image of an organization was a big machine cranking out products, the new image is the Internet and the web. The Internet consists of routers, servers, data hubs, and other advanced telecommunications equipment. As such, the Internet is the contemporary equivalent of the big industrial companies of the last century: it needs to be highly efficient and supremely reliable. The web, in contrast, is the infinitely interconnected network of data and knowledge that flows through the Internet. It symbolizes the way in which contemporary organizations need to be fluid, open, flexible, and almost continuously experimental and recombinant.

The final reason why lateral accountability creates difficult struggles for leaders needs little elaboration. A market-driven, recombinant world is uncertain and often turbulent. As a result, leaders have to respond to surprises, shocks, and opportunities—at the same time they are working hard to meet specific, often stringent demands, working under close monitoring, sharing authority with powerful, mobile parties, and trying to comprehend and manage very complex organizations.

How difficult is the struggle to meet the demands of lateral accountability? One indication is the high rate of failure of even the best funded, best managed, and best supported entrepreneurial ventures. The new invisible hand puts organizations on a high wire. Many fall off and find no safety net on the way down.

The other indication is the toll that lateral accountability exacts from leaders. Entrepreneurs' work often becomes their lives. They sacrifice a great deal for what they accomplish. This is sometimes explained as simply the challenge of doing everything needed to build a new organization or create a new product or service. But closer examination shows that the demands of responsible leadership in an entrepreneurial world result, fundamentally, from meeting the demands of multiple, exacting markets under conditions of intense competitive pressure, high uncertainty, and scarce resources—the basic features of a market-driven recombinant economy. Resources are not locked in—the individuals and groups who control them can move them elsewhere fairly quickly, and this makes new organizations fragile. They are assembled quickly and can be disassembled quickly.

In the giant, stable, powerful corporate machines of the last century, leaders had the time, resources, and staff to analyze, negotiate, and manage evolving relationships. For the most part, these relationships changed slowly and predictably. All that is much less common today, even for leaders in large, established firms. In a fluid, uncertain, continuously recombinant world, making good on a set of simultaneous commitments is an all-encompassing challenge that often feels like an unremitting struggle. This is a profoundly challenging prospect, so why should capable men and women take it on?

Flourishing

The answer to this question lies, in part, in a surprising connection between a very old idea and the thinking of many entrepreneurs today. If someone asks an entrepreneur why he or she is pouring so much of himself or herself into a hard, uncertain effort, the answer often involves what the entrepreneur is trying to build or create. Sometimes this is a product or a service, and sometimes it is a particular kind of organization. Near the end of his career, for example, Steve Jobs said that his greatest pride wasn't the remarkable products he helped develop but the lasting company he built, something his personal heroes, Bill Hewlett and David Packard, had done in creating Hewlett-Packard.[13]

The old idea is Aristotle's. The capsule version of it is "flourishing."[14] Aristotle's basic reason why men and women should lead virtuous lives is that they and their communities would flourish if they did so. Today, a flourishing organization is a strong, growing, vibrant human community, and a flourishing company is a splendid, extraordinarily complex human creation—valuable in itself and also for what it does for others.

When leaders help create thriving, successful organizations, they are achieving something of profound human value. A flourishing organization is a source of jobs, training, personal development, tax revenue for communities, new products and services, pride, and meaning—along with a stream of profits that benefit a multitude of investors. Unfortunately, many communities around the world have learned, often painfully, how valuable flourishing companies are because their local companies have lost ground, moved operations to lower-cost locations, or gone out of business. Struggling successfully to create, build, and lead a thriving business is a remarkable, difficult, and valuable act of human creativity and social contribution. Men and women who do this, or simply attempt it, are directly and deeply engaged in the good struggle.

Today, in a turbulent world, a flourishing organization is a fragile creature. In a multimarket world, it takes hard, dedicated, endless work by a leader and a senior management team to build and defend a strong, vital organization. When leaders meet this challenge, they should have a sense of well-earned pride, and they merit serious respect. David Lilienthal, who ran the Tennessee Valley Authority for twenty years and then headed the Atomic Energy Commission, once wrote, "The managerial life is the broadest, the most demanding, and by all odds the most comprehensive and subtle of all human activities."

Its aim, he believed, was "to lead and move and bring out the latent capabilities—and dreams—of other human beings."[15]

What responsible leaders also understand is that demanding standards of accountability can actually make their organizations stronger. Some entrepreneurs seek "dumb money" so they have more freedom to do what they want. But dumb money can be very expensive because it robs a leader and an organization of the knowledge, experience, guidance, and occasional "tough love" provided by intelligent, experienced, vigilant outsiders.

Business leaders often have an ambivalent view of markets. Free markets enable them to introduce new products and services, create new businesses, and expand geographically. But as markets get more competitive, profits fall and their jobs get harder. This is why the giant twentieth-century firms devised so many ways—cartels, protectionism, regulatory capture, tacit arrangements on price and capacity expansion, and the like—to moderate and control markets. The great industrial statesmen of the twentieth century often worked hard to manage or reduce competitive pressures on their firms.

In a dynamic, recombinant economy, far-sighted and courageous leaders will work hard to shed the twentieth-century strategic preoccupation with blocking and managing competitive pressure. Instead, they will ask which market pressures their firms should actively seek out in order to strengthen them for the long run. This is something entrepreneurial firms do routinely, because they have no choice. These companies typically must succeed against large, established competitors and compete hard for customers, suppliers, and funding. Intense competitive pressure often strengthens these companies.

The courageous questions for responsible leaders today ask: What sharply defined commitments do I want to make to other parties that will make me and my organization struggle hard and creatively? How can I use markets to strengthen and reinforce the aims and standards I have set for my organization? What forms of accountability can I develop, in collaboration with other market actors, to create the right pressures and expectations for myself and my organization? Behind these questions is the basic view that organizations, like individuals, can grow stronger and flourish because of the conditions, pressures, and incentives they confront.

All too often, leaders seek buffers from external pressures. The courageous path is creating a customized form of accountability that puts the right pressures and expectations on an organization by making commitments that say the organization will struggle vigorously and creatively to accomplish certain, specific outcomes for certain, specific groups. This means asking, To which groups will we be acutely responsible? What specifically will we commit to doing for these groups? How transparent and candid will we be, to enable markets to assess and react to what we do and fail to do? What pressures, scrutiny, and risks do we want to create or invite in order to build a strong, resilient, responsible organization?

For responsible leaders today, accountability isn't an obligation in a rulebook or a lawyer's brief or a regulatory document. And, because markets are fallible and manipulable, leaders cannot simply equate market performance with meeting their responsibilities. Accountability is, to a significant degree, a set of standards that leaders create for themselves. It is something leaders play a significant role in defining and then shaping and reshaping. As a result, for responsible leaders, the fundamental question is, What strong mutual commitments do we want to create, above and beyond the systems of accountability we are required to comply with, that will create the most valuable and exciting opportunities for my organization?

But once leaders have made the commitments that define their accountability, another set of demanding challenges looms: this is the challenge of making critical decisions in ways that clearly reflect how a leader and an organization have defined their accountability. We turn to this challenge next.

CHAPTER FOUR

HOW DO I MAKE CRITICAL DECISIONS?

The third enduring question of responsible leadership asks, How do I make critical decisions? This is a universal question of leadership, and men and women who have had real responsibility can all recall situations—often in vivid, wrenching detail—in which they had to make decisions that would truly shape their organizations or even decide their fates.

Critical decisions have always involved struggle, commitment, and courage. For business leaders, mistakes can mean hardship for hundreds or thousands of people and the end of long-cherished dreams. Getting major decisions right can mean jobs, opportunity, confidence, hope for many people, and a sense of pride and accomplishment for leaders. Leaders need inner strength to face these decisions straight on, see the facts and uncertainties for what they are, commit one way or another, and then follow through doggedly, for months or years, to get the implementation right.

During the last century, the large industrial companies developed a distinctive way for leaders to make critical decisions and raise the odds of success. This approach reflected the practices of successful leaders of this era and the distinctive challenges they faced. Methodical analysis and corporate power were central: the analysis helped leaders make the right decisions, and power reduced risks.

The rise and fall of many of the great organizations of the last century is also the story of the rise and fall of this way of making major decisions. This classic approach reflected a particular type of important decision—a strategic investment in a large manufacturing plant—but it became a template for making many types of critical choices. The template has been enormously valuable, but now, with the rise of the new invisible hand, it is fading in importance.

A new approach may be emerging and may help responsible managers get critical decisions right, but it provides no guarantees and involves real hazards. To see why, it is important to understand the classic approach to critical decisions and to understand, in particular, how it helped managers make sound decisions and, in turn, create unprecedented wealth for their organizations and their societies.

The Twentieth-Century Template

General Motors was started by an entrepreneur, William Crapo "Billy" Durant. With vision, charm, and a buccaneering spirit, Durant aggregated dozens of automakers and suppliers into General Motors. But he couldn't manage the sprawling entity he created, and he lost control of it in 1920. His successor, Alfred Sloan, was a brilliant organizational architect and systematizer. He developed decision processes that helped make the company one of the largest and most profitable firms in history. By the middle of the last century, the company was a paragon of management excellence.

For Sloan and most other twentieth-century business leaders, a critical, recurring decision was determining when and how to build a large new factory. The most famous American examples are Henry Ford's decision to build the vast River Rouge plant, the series of investments by Andrew Carnegie in ever-larger and more dominant steel mills, and IBM's historic investment in developing and manufacturing the 360 series of computers.

When leaders got the "big factory" decision right, they created an extraordinary virtuous circle. The more a factory produced, the less it cost to make each additional unit. This was because its fixed costs were spread over more units, and more output meant more experience and more learning about better and less costly ways to manufacture. The profits from a large, modern plant, running at full capacity, could then be invested in newer technology and additional capacity. This meant a company could move from strength to strength. On the other hand, when leaders got the "big factory" decision wrong, they destroyed companies or had to lug a costly ball and chain for many years.

Because decisions about "the big factory" were often bet-the-firm and bet-my-career choices, executives developed two ways to reduce risk and uncertainty. The first was methodical analysis. In general, this involved several basic steps. The process started by setting out the basic options for dealing with an important issue. Then staff members and middle managers, sometimes assisted by external consultants, produced detailed analyses of each option. Next, senior management discussed the analysis in detail. Then the CEO or senior leadership teams made a final decision. This was followed by the final step of actual implementation. Different parts of an organization were assigned responsibility for projects, and ultimately individuals were assigned specific tasks. The decision, in Peter Drucker's phrase, had "degenerat[ed] into work."[1]

In reality, of course, decision making was messier than this, but the ideal of a rational, methodical, strategic approach to the hardest challenges facing an organization was extraordinarily powerful. In fact, it seemed to have universal applicability, and well-managed military, government, religious, and nonprofit organizations generally followed some version of it. At its worst, this way of making critical decisions was slow, bureaucratic, inward looking, and political. At its best, it was comprehensive, evidence based, and strategy driven.

But even at its best, this decision process left business leaders with significant risks because the best analysis could not foretell the future. As a result, leaders took a second step, when they could, to reduce their risks: they worked hard to create stable, predictable, even controlled environments around their companies. Put differently, they followed the adage, "The best way to predict the future is to control it."

GM was an exemplar of this approach, but many other firms used similar tactics. They sought control over suppliers, through backward integration and multiple sourcing, to ensure steady, secure, low-cost raw materials. They first fought labor unions, then tried to co-opt them, and sometimes fled them through outsourcing to stabilize their labor supply and minimize its cost. They sought power over customers through retail price maintenance, branding, control of distribution channels, and sometimes outright collusion with competitors. They retained earnings and limited debt to reduce dependence on bankers and financial markets. And they used lobbying and stakeholder management to limit competition.

Each of these tactics helped reduce the risk and uncertainty of large investments by creating more stable, predictable, even malleable environments around companies. The idea underlying this approach was powerfully articulated by Professor Michael Porter in *Competitive Strategy*, one of the most important works on strategy in the twentieth century. Its central idea was that a successful strategy blocked or neutralized the competitive forces surrounding a firm. If a company failed to do this, other parties—suppliers, customers, competitors, and new entrants, for example—would erode its profits.

Corporate power is sometimes equated with evil, but business leaders who relied on methodical planning, large-scale manufacturing operations, and managed environments were often acting responsibly and making valuable social contributions because this approach to critical decisions translated the brilliant fusion of knowledge, power, and accountability into reality. The insiders who dominated the decision process really understood the organization, its technology, and its markets, employees, and production systems. They also understood the politics of the organization and knew how to get things done. And these senior executives could act decisively on what they knew because they sat at the top of strong hierarchies.

From society's point of view, the leaders and senior teams could be held accountable for how they used their information and their power through the vertical governance system of boards of directors, laws and regulation, and democratic mandates. The giant manufacturing machines contributed immensely to the physical well-being of billions of people. When they ran full and steady, the huge organizational machines produced historically unprecedented torrents of cars, refrigerators, oil, gasoline, and ultimately drugs and computers. And these companies—or at least the ones that survived—succeeded in steadily raising the quality of their products and steadily lowering their prices.

Unfortunately, however, the success of this decision system—the co-evolution of sophisticated internal analysis and external market and political power—led to vulnerability and even failure. Perhaps the strongest evidence for the power of markets today is the demise of so many once impregnable corporate citadels. Part of the problem was that profits and power enabled these firms to create ever more elaborate planning and management systems. These made them inward looking and sluggish, and their once-valuable stakeholders relations ossified and locked them into indefensible competitive positions. Then new waves of competition exploited these vulnerabilities. Some came from entrepreneurial firms that grew large and powerful, such as the Japanese carmakers that bested their American competitors. Other competition came from new constellations of smaller firms, such as the fluid alliances that transformed the computer industry and nearly bankrupted IBM.

But this is only the most familiar part of the story. The forces that undermined the great corporate bastions are the basic forces of a recombinant economy. They are weakening the brilliant fusion of knowledge, power, and responsibility and making the classic approach to making critical decisions much less effective.

The Challenge Today

The brilliant fusion worked because the dominant companies of the last century could develop and control most of the knowledge they needed to build strong, competitive businesses. This made their leaders and their hierarchies powerful, and boards of directors and government could hold them accountable for how they used their knowledge and power. But all that has now changed, and the reason is the clichéd phrase "the knowledge explosion." Now even a huge R&D department, staffed with leading engineers, technicians, and even Nobel laureate scientists, cannot develop all the knowledge a company needs. For example, after IBM research developed the "Watson" system of artificial intelligence—made famous by its televised victory over two all-time "Jeopardy" champions—the next step was finding commercial applications. To develop information services for doctors, IBM created an alliance with Columbia Medical School and Nuance Corporation, a leading voice recognition company.

The knowledge companies need to succeed today often resides in other companies and organizations, and these organizations are typically players in competitive markets and are engaged in their own efforts to succeed through creative recombinations. Both Columbia Medical School and Nuance, for example, have a multitude of alliances with other organizations. In other words, knowledge critical to an organization can reside anywhere: in a home country or around the globe; inside competitors, suppliers, or customers; or in universities, government laboratories, joint ventures, and other alliances and consortia.

This knowledge doesn't repose quietly in these organizations, like library books on an immense, global shelf.

Most of these organizations are active players in markets. These markets are continuously churning, and they create a wide range of options for selling or bartering knowledge. This gives power to the organizations most effective at developing knowledge. And this, in turn, dramatically weakens the power of leaders and companies that need this knowledge. A world of markets is a world of options, with very different relationships between knowledge and power. As knowledge disperses, power disperses.

This gives "outsiders" power to influence, shape, and sometimes even dominate decisions made "inside" an organization. As a result, few leaders today are working in stable, quasi-managed external environments. Their organizations are surrounded by a vast array of competitors and other organizations pursuing their own interests in multiple markets. The interactions among these parties are hard to predict, much less control. Because the competitive world is now a vast multiplayer interactive game, familiar ways of making critical decisions and reducing risk and uncertainty are much less useful. Even highly sophisticated new tools, such as the risk models used by the large banks at the center of the global financial crisis, have been overwhelmed by complexity, uncertainty, and unexpected interactions.

As a result, the twentieth-century template for critical decisions—reducing the risk of "big factory" commitments through methodical analysis and corporate power—is becoming less effective. Modern economies are knowledge economies, so many companies never build plants, and firms that need manufacturing can now "rent" the big factory rather than design it, build it, and run it themselves. And outsourcing does more than lower cost. It also creates "option value" in an uncertain world. Depending on what the future brings, companies can move to other suppliers and find better prices, products, or logistics. Some firms still choose to own manufacturing for strategic reasons, but the classic, massive, one-time investment in fixed assets, long-term employment, and stable stakeholder relationships is giving way to ever-shifting networks of temporary arrangements. As a result, the paradigm for important decisions is changing significantly.

As knowledge and power disperse and as risk and uncertainty rise, leaders now need new ways to meet their central responsibility of getting critical decisions right. They need to move beyond the thinking of important decisions as once-and-for-all, long-term choices among high-stakes, well-defined options. This type of decision has by no means disappeared, but it is increasingly an outdated template for understanding leaders' important decisions. The familiar tactic of methodical planning, implemented in a benign, quasi-managed environment of corporate power, is no longer a sound guide to making important decisions.

In response, a different approach to making critical decisions is emerging, with distinct hazards and opportunities for responsible leaders. This new approach reflects the world of entrepreneurs. They live with intensely competitive, often turbulent markets—a far cry from the buffer zones and spheres of influence surrounding the large twentieth-century hierarchical organizations. Entrepreneurs have to make these decisions with scant information, little or no staff to do detailed analysis, no budget for consultants, scarce time for decisions, and little room for error.

Evolving Commitments

In a recombinant world, responsible leaders can hardly abandon the classic approach to critical decisions. Analysis still matters—even if it only produces rough estimates, broad parameters, and ranges of possibilities—because the alternative of operating on instinct is reckless when the stakes and uncertainties are high. And bosses haven't disappeared and won't, because someone still needs to make final decisions. Napoleon's adage that "One bad general is better than two good ones" continues to reflect important lessons about human nature and effective leadership.[2]

There is, however, a powerful reason for an alternative approach in turbulent, uncertain, market-driven environments: in essence, there is a great deal that leaders cannot anticipate, and some surprises can be deadly. During his early years, when John D. Rockefeller was just another unknown oil field entrepreneur, he gave himself a nightly sermon with the reminder, "But suppose the oil fields ran out."[3] More than a century later, other entrepreneurs had similar worldviews. Andy Grove, one of the founders of Intel, is famous for saying, "Only the para-noid survive."[4] And Herb Kelleher, the founder of South-west Airlines, was once said to have forecast eleven of the last three recessions, because he was so vigilant about the risks to his company.[5] In fact, empirical studies suggest that pessimistic entrepreneurs outperform their optimistic counterparts.[6]

In a turbulent, sometimes dangerous world, responsi-ble leaders need a broader view of critical decisions. This means viewing these decisions as commitments, but in an unconventional way. We typically think of commitments as deep, abiding pledges that individuals and organiza-tions will do absolutely all they can to make good on. In contrast, the kind of commitments that matter critically today are paradoxical: they are evolving commitments.

An evolving commitment is a pledge, by a leader and an organization, to move in a particular direction, but to do so in a flexible, open-ended way. High-stakes, high-risk, once-and-for-all decisions—the contemporary ver-sions of the "big factory" decisions—are sometimes unavoidable, but evolving commitments are far better suited to a world in which leaders are immersed in a stream of possibilities, surprises, opportunities, and deals in the active, fluid markets that surround and pervade their organizations. Commitments require data, analysis, and experienced judgment, but, all too often, these are far from decisive.

In more and more cases, when leaders make critical decisions, they are not choosing among specific, detailed options, each supported by in-depth analysis, nor are they expecting to implement the option they choose in a familiar, predictable, or managed environment. All they are doing is making an initial choice, for themselves and their organizations, among broad, flexible, open-ended directions. This initial direction will evolve, sometimes dramatically, in response to what is learned from first steps, hard-to-predict developments in the churning, recombinant markets around companies, and reactions in the markets for funding, talent, partners, and meaning.

Evolving commitments have always been central to entrepreneurial success. Leaders of new organizations have never been able to see very far into the future. They have usually been surrounded by intensely competitive, often turbulent markets—a far cry from the buffer zones and spheres of influence surrounding the large twentieth-century hierarchical organizations. They typically didn't know whether their product would work, what it would really cost to make and sell it on a large scale, whether a large, established firm would copy it or use influence with government to create obstacles, whether other entrepreneurs were on the brink of introducing something similar or better, and whether they would even have enough cash to operate beyond a few months.

Under conditions like these, all a responsible leader can do is whatever analysis is possible, commit to moving in a particular direction, carefully plan the immediate next steps, work hard to learn from execution and experiment, seize opportunities along the way, and be prepared to recalibrate an organization's efforts, again and again, to match emerging realities. Decision making has to be as fluid as the markets around an organization.

Instead of periodic big decisions, responsible leaders make or orchestrate an unending series of smaller ones—all aimed at some larger, broad, flexible objective. Gary Mueller, the founder of ISI Emerging Markets, which provides hard-to-get information on companies in emerging markets, said, "You have to make decisions because indecision is a decision. So you say this is the direction we're going in, but you're constantly asking if you're doing the right thing and adjusting what you're doing."[7]

In a world of heightened hazards and uncertainty, leaders who make commitments to other parties are basically saying, "This is the overall direction we plan to pursue and this is what we specifically plan to do and accomplish in the near future, but a lot will change, perhaps dramatically."

Commitments are serious pledges. They have real legal and ethical weight, and responsible leaders and their organizations work very hard to make good on them, but these commitments, in a recombinant world, are inescapably flexible and fallible. The bolder the initiative or the more turbulent the environment, the more appropriate and inevitable these types of commitments are.

From a broader perspective, an organization today is not simply what Michael Jensen and William Meckling called—in an insightful and widely cited phrase—a "nexus of contracts."[8] It is also a nexus of commitments, and sophisticated parties understand this from the start. There is often too much uncertainty and turbulence in market-driven economies to rely on contracts and contingencies to specify who will do what and when. Without ongoing, flexible adaptation, entrepreneurs and the market actors who support them would have only one shot at success, and this would typically be a shot in the dark, given the many uncertainties new ventures face.[9]

Evolving commitments are basically the managerial version of a longstanding view of military strategy. Almost two centuries ago, Carl von Clausewitz, the brilliant Prussian general and strategist, wrote, "War is an area of uncertainty; three quarters of the things on which all action in war is based lie in a fog of uncertainty to a greater or lesser extent."[10] His view was that the principal value of careful military planning was to prepare a force for the first engagement with the enemy and little more. It is no coincidence that some entrepreneurs today echo Clausewitz's observation and say the purpose of a business plan is to prepare a new organization for its first engagement with a customer. In other words, entrepreneurs can raise their chances of success by gathering data, studying customers and their industry, trying to assess likely competitor moves, and trying to understand where and how they can best focus their limited resources. At the same time, however, they have to keep their thinking loose, broad, flexible, and revisable.

Next Right Steps

Leaders rely on evolving commitments for three practical reasons. First, they can. Knowledge-based organizations are more flexible than traditional manufacturing firms with dedicated factories, and firms that sell products today can rely on outsourcing and flexible factories to "produce" them. Second, they often have to. A wide range of actors are typically involved in monitoring and shaping an organization's decisions; these parties want a say in what the organization does, and their own agendas are continuously evolving in response to the continuously shifting, sometimes turbulent markets around them.

The third and most important reason for leaders to rely on evolving commitments is that they should. Responsible decisions should not outrun visibility, and, in a recombinant world, it is hard to see much of the future. In addition, there is a great deal to be learned from execution, experiment, and actual experience. Finally, going step by step provides people inside an organization and all the parties in the multiple markets around it with clear, immediate objectives and even metrics.

This enables all these parties to concentrate their efforts, focus on meeting specific objectives, and not be paralyzed by endless possibilities. The greater the uncertainty, the more important it is for leaders to provide a clear path, even if it is almost certain to be adjusted and readjusted, to enable others to commit, plan, and work with a strong sense of confidence.

What counts as a "right next step"? It is a task, a project, or an assignment that is clearly defined, doable, and has a significant probability of contributing to a larger, longer-term aim—as that aim is currently defined. The right next step, in many cases, also takes two lessons from modern finance. First, it opens up options for subsequent steps. Second, it gets the risks right. In other words, high-risk, low-reward activities—however bold and exciting they may sound—are rarely the right next step.

In addition, in a knowledge-based world, the right next step often serves as an experiment. That is, it creates knowledge that can be used to plan subsequent steps or even test and adjust the larger aim. The great industrial companies of the last century developed long-term strategies and sought to execute them as efficiently as possible. Now, in a knowledge-based economy, "execution as learning" is becoming much more important.[11]

A clear example of this approach is the staged investments that venture capital firms make in new businesses. Each round of investment depends on whether an entrepreneur and an organization have met a set of shorter-term objectives and metrics. If they haven't, they need persuasive explanations of what happened, what they would do differently the next time, and why another approach is likely to work better. The critical challenge in many successful entrepreneurial ventures is repeatedly hitting a series of short-term targets under the pressure of limited cash, close scrutiny from market players, and a serious prospect that failure will reduce financing or lead to new leadership or both.

The "next right step" approach reflects the observation of Professor Lynda Applegate, who has studied and worked with entrepreneurs for three decades. She said, "All I know is that many initial assumptions are wrong, and the questions that must be answered are, how important is the assumption to the success of the business, how can I experiment to learn more, and are there other options I could pursue?"[12]

In short, the bold, strategic decision maker is giving way to the responsible, intensely committed orchestrator, pragmatist, and deal maker. These men and women are skilled at seeing patterns in the fluid markets around them and working with a wide range of parties to adapt, shift, and recombine, all against the background of a broad strategic direction. More broadly, responsibility is becoming a hard-to-forecast trajectory. Commitments evolve, like a perpetual campaign or a floating craps game, as leaders strike a series of bargains with a range of different parties in a wide range of markets and then make good on these bargains or fail to do so. In either event, they then make new commitments and bargains, and the cycle of commitment and adaptation continues.

Faith, Humility, and Restraint

When leaders rely on evolving commitments to make critical decisions, they have to wrestle with a hard problem, one that challenges them intellectually, emotionally, and pragmatically. And it is a surprising problem, because it involves two traits—faith and humility—more typically associated with religion than business and management.

Responsible leadership in a turbulent, entrepreneurial world involves a deep commitment to an imagined future. Shikhar Ghosh, who has served as the founder, CEO, or chairman of eight technology-based entrepreneurial companies, described the commitment this way:

> *You need a core of faith. This faith matters to the organization and the entrepreneur. Entrepreneurs have to believe so they filter away contrary information. They have to be the driving force and so they see things and present things in the best possible light. In a new company, the basic proposition is in doubt at all times, and you're also asking for a lot of sacrifice from everyone. You have to convince yourself and feel you are honest about your belief, because you can't feel like a liar and convince others.*[13]

Faith is a deep confidence that an opportunity is real, that a leader and team have the skills to seize it, and that success in this effort matters profoundly. This faith underlies the broad range of commitments that leaders make and helps them move forward in the face of inevitable adversity, disappointment, frustration, and a high chance of failure, and it enables others to do the same. Entrepreneurial activity, in companies of all sizes and in all organizations, always involves a leap of faith, a deep personal commitment to an imagined future. Robert

Higgins, the cofounder and general partner of Highland Capital Partners, observed, "People are deciding whether or not to buy a belief."[14]

Faith and deep commitment are crucial from the earliest stages of an evolving commitment, because commitments evolve and can fail at many points along the way. Leaders need the courage to face ongoing uncertainty, what at times feels like overwhelming complexity, and—no matter how high their hopes—a decent prospect of failure. Committing an organization to a particular direction—with a full, imagined understanding of what success and failure, for the leader and others who depend on an organization for their livelihoods, could mean and the inevitability of surprises and frustrations—takes real courage.

Uncertainty and fluidity create opportunity but also bring the real and ever-present prospect of failure. This is particularly true when a leader and an organization are committed to a path that significantly departs from the conventional wisdom. The fear of failure is easily intensified by the mental and physical stress of the job. When many of an organization's critical assets are mobile, leaders need to be vigilant and active to avoid losing them. When competition is tough and returns are low, organizations are more fragile and vulnerable, as are leaders' jobs. When the decision process is continuous and involves outside parties and partners, new complexities arise. All these can make leadership and decision making a long slog, which is why commitment and everyday determination and courage are central for responsible leadership today.

The risk of deep, faith-based commitments is that they will keep a leader focused on a specific goal and a way of achieving it, regardless of what is happening around him or her. Stopped clocks are correct twice a day, but are badly wrong the rest of the time. So what keeps an intense commitment from being a private, compelling, and ultimately futile fantasy?

Shikhar Ghosh explained how to reconcile faith in a vision with realism with a surprising metaphor. "Entrepreneurs are like guerrilla fighters," he said. "They know the odds of defeating the enemy are low and that the casualty rate will be high and the jungle is miserable, but they have a gut belief that they can win and, more important, like guerrilla fighters, they are constantly adapting to what they experience and learn."[15]

Responsible leadership in a market-driven world demands commitment to a vision and core values—as well as a complex form of self-management, in which humility and restraint play a critical role. Leaders have to simultaneously understand what is really happening around them and respond to this reality, while remaining deeply committed to longer-term and possibly evanescent possibilities. This is, perhaps, the fundamental, underlying, pervasive struggle for responsible leaders today. Faith can blind leaders to reality, but reality can eviscerate faith. Responsible leaders need both and hence must live and work with the permanent tension between them.

In the middle of the global financial crisis, the CEO of a major bank was listening to a young banker present an analysis of a complex portfolio of securities. At one point, the CEO interrupted and asked whether they were talking about the difference of 15 percent or 15 basis points. With his question, the CEO revealed to everyone in the room how little he understood about at least one aspect of the presentation.

What is striking about this story is that the CEO had an extraordinary record of accomplishment and successfully guided his bank through the crisis. He was also widely viewed as an extremely intelligent, hands-on executive. Nevertheless, he was willing to show everyone in the room that, even though he was a "master of the universe," as Tom Wolfe memorably described investment bankers in *The Bonfire of the Vanities,* there were things the CEO didn't understand and wasn't embarrassed to ask about. By doing this, he set a valuable example of the courage of humility and restraint.

These two traits are particularly important for making critical decisions responsibly, particularly when these decisions are evolving commitments and the men and women making them are struggling with intense, always-on accountability and market pressures. Humility is an attitude that reflects how little leaders sometimes know about the complex, uncertain world surrounding them. Restraint then takes humility and puts it into practice. It means moving patiently, carefully, and analytically, rather than boldly and confidently.

This may be a surprising perspective on making critical decisions. A common but misleading view of entrepreneurs sees them as courageous because they eagerly embrace critical, high-stakes, high-risk decisions and then move forward, boldly and fearlessly. In other words, entrepreneurs are unfazed by the risks of critical decisions and even eager to take them on. But this romantic view has two serious problems.

First, it fails Aristotle's classic test of courage. He didn't simply ask if a leader was moving ahead boldly. His question was whether a leader was balancing boldness with prudence, because ignoring or courting risk and danger is mere recklessness. For Aristotle, courage was a golden mean, a hard-to-achieve midpoint between the hazardous extremes of reckless bravado and enervating caution. In other words, serious commitment is revealed in calibration and, over the long haul, requires frequent adjustment to maintain a balanced approach and avoid dangerous extremes. Aristotle was hardly alone in thinking this way. In the Eastern tradition, the *Tao De Ching,* an ancient Chinese text that served as a foundation for both Buddhism and Taoism, says, "Whoever is stiff and inflexible is a disciple of death. Whoever is soft and yielding is a disciple of life."[16]

This classic perspective is confirmed by contemporary observations of successful entrepreneurs. The familiar charge-the-hill view of these men and women distorts how they actually think about risk. Entrepreneurs may have more tolerance for risk than big-company executives, but the reality is that successful entrepreneurs, in both big and small organizations, assess risk carefully, assume it only if the payoff seems right, and then look for ways to reduce or share the risks without significantly changing the payoff.

Why are modesty and restraint particularly valuable in an entrepreneurial world? The basic reason is that they help leaders address an uncomfortable but central challenge to success: their significant, inevitable, and ever-growing ignorance. The faster the world changes and the more complex it becomes, the less anyone—including the most brilliantly endowed leaders—really understands what is going on around them and understands what the future will bring.

Humility and restraint help remedy the challenge of ignorance in several ways. First, they encourage leaders to open their eyes and learn all they can. The bold, self-designated geniuses who have compelling visions of the future are much less likely to listen sensitively and observe acutely. In contrast, leaders who understand that they have few of the answers—and sometimes don't know if the answer is 15 percent or 15 basis points—are more likely to really understand that others around them, inside and outside their organizations, can hold critical puzzle pieces. An evolving commitment is, simultaneously, a decision process and a learning process for leaders and organizations, and modesty and restraint accelerate their learning.

Humility and restraint also encourage leaders to "buy insurance" against their ignorance, fallibility, and risks.

This insurance isn't free, but it protects other people, to a degree, against harm and suffering in the event of bad surprises. This insurance can take several different forms. It involves trying hard to break big decisions into small phases and using each phase as an experiment and a learning opportunity. It means going step by patient step, rather than by leaps and bounds, and disclosing results to others to get feedback. It means trying hard to avoid committing much further than a leader can actually see. And it means remaining vigilant for surprises, problems, and opportunities to accelerate efforts.

"Buying insurance" even means relying on a widely criticized way of making decisions—by taking a short-term and finance-oriented perspective on them, both of which are important to making calibrated, evolving commitments. The short-term focus asks who needs to do what as clear, doable, but initial steps toward making good on a larger, longer-term aim. At the same time, it means asking a basic question from modern finance, What options will these initial steps create and what options will they foreclose?

This is the reason start-up firms are strongly advised to conserve their cash, because cash is an all-purpose insurance policy against surprises. A few financial service firms "bought insurance" before the financial crisis by reducing leverage and limiting their reliance on real estate–based securities. In the short term, this hurt their earnings and their stock prices. But in the longer term, this insurance helped them survive. But options aren't solely financial. In fact, the crucial ones are options to experiment, learn, recalibrate, modify commitments, and open up new options.

The histories of the great entrepreneurs show them working patiently and persistently, and often struggling to grasp what they don't know yet badly need to know to make good on their vision. John D. Rockefeller and Andrew Carnegie are now often remembered as industrial titans presiding over the vast empires known as Standard Oil and U.S. Steel. But they began their careers as entrepreneurs, building businesses in an era at least as turbulent, confusing, and dangerous as ours today.

What the two men had in common was the same approach to dealing with the complex and constantly shifting fundamentals in their industries—and, perhaps, with the anxieties and fears they felt. They gathered the best hard data they could, though it was often scant, and then they immersed themselves in whatever uncertainties were critical to their businesses and worked relentlessly to understand the areas of uncertainty, analyze them, and get a feel for how they might evolve.

Rockefeller's crucial insight—that the chaotically entrepreneurial world of the emerging oil industry needed a systemic solution—came only after a long period of what one biographer called his "exhaustive study" of the industry and countless hours in the oil fields.[17] Carnegie paid acute attention to the details of cost and production in the iron industry and the embryonic steel industry. He was often credited with almost supernatural insight into industry trends, but his authoritative biographer viewed

this talent as the result of a wide network of industry con-
tacts that Carnegie cultivated and his willingness to work
the network intensively.[18]

In all likelihood, neither Rockefeller nor Carnegie
would be known today if they had succumbed to the
widespread myth that successful entrepreneurs rely heavily on passionate commitments and brilliant insights into
the future. This runs completely contrary to the experience of veteran entrepreneurs and those who fund them.
Professor Howard Stevenson, whose career involved
forty years of studying, working with, and investing in
entrepreneurs, observed, "Ninety percent of the crazy
passionate entrepreneurs that I've seen end up failing."[19]

This approach to critical decisions—relying on evolving commitments, humility, and restraint—can feel more
like shirking responsibility than taking it, and it can feel
deeply unsettling to individuals who think that leaders
are supposed to be bosses, making big decisions and then
pushing their aggressive implementation. But in an uncertain, fluid world, the most responsible approach to a
big decision is often delaying or trying to break it down
into smaller decisions—to keep options open, reduce the
risk of any single decision, and learn as much as possible
from experience and experiment and from a wide range
of parties inside and outside an organization.

Put differently, what responsible leaders often need
today is the courage to make "bad decisions"—at least as
viewed from the twentieth-century perspective. These are
short term, provisional, and open to revision. They are

the best bets available for moving an organization in the right direction, in the face of what mathematical modelers call "computationally intractable" problems. This is a world that often resembles a giant pinball machine: events in one market surrounding a firm can trigger complicated chains of events in other markets, and then these events can trigger still others.

The only real antidote to these hazards is making critical decisions with humility and restraint. This is the spirit of the traditional prayer of Breton fishermen, "O God, the sea is so vast and my boat is so small."[20] Sometimes, fallibility means things work out better or differently than expected. Sometimes, it means missing warnings and dangers because everything looks good. But getting critical decisions right, when they take the form of evolving commitments, is particularly challenging.

In the end, leaders make the important decisions, and this is their responsibility. But they do so at various points in a long process of evolving commitments that responsible leaders shape and guide with both a compelling, exciting, sometimes bold direction and the courage to move forward, despite abiding vulnerability, and to act with prudence, humility, and restraint.

Waiting for New Truisms

Organizations still need "bosses"; the buck will continue to stop on their desks, and at times leaders will make the big calls. But these familiar truisms now give only a partial view of how responsible leaders make critical decisions.

New truisms, suited to the era of the new invisible hand, haven't emerged, but they will most likely measure leaders not by the standard of the bold, inspiring, and far-sighted final decision maker, but as insightful, strategic, intensely committed orchestrators. These leaders "make" many important decisions by guiding fluid, evolving, varied, customized processes involving a wide range of parties both inside their company and in the intensely competitive, recombinant markets surrounding them.

What responsibility now requires is a broader view of the decision process when an important decision must be made, as well as a wider repertory of skills. Leaders need to see themselves less often as bosses and more often as the spiders at the center of a web, sensing and responding to developments in a wide range of ways. Managing a network of knowledge workers is different from building the big factory and then running it full and steady.

Responsible decision making today is a demanding struggle that requires almost continuous observing, questioning, learning, forgetting, negotiating, and adjusting—all in a climate of pressure, uncertainty, surprises, and basic fallibility. Doing this well requires a sound answer to the enduring question of how to make critical decisions and to another enduring question as well. That question—which asks about an organization's real values—is the subject of the next chapter. If a hierarchy of bosses isn't available to oversee the implementation of a large, once-and-for-all decision, the values of an organization will determine how well it makes good on its commitments and whether it succeeds or fails.

CHAPTER FIVE

DO WE HAVE THE RIGHT CORE VALUES?

It is easy to be skeptical about values today. At best, they express ideals and principles that leaders and organizations really care about. But often they are just vague phrases that float in the ether, far above messy problems, and sometimes values even serve as camouflage for corruption. Enron, for example, had a lofty mission statement and a long list of explicit organizational values. So perhaps the skeptics are right.

On the other hand, great leaders have always cared deeply about values. They believed in the power of values to inspire effort and sacrifice and to shape hopes, dreams, and behavior, even years or decades after a leader was gone. Great leaders also understood that values help everyone, including themselves, answer profound questions about the larger aims of work, life, and society. What should we really care about? What do all our efforts count for in the long run? What are good ways for people to live and work with each other? How should leaders use their power?

Today, values matter for another reason: they may be the only force that can counter the power of markets and market-based thinking. This makes the fourth enduring question—Do we have the right core values?—especially important. Responsible leaders need to think hard about values and do this in the context of the pervasive markets of the new invisible hand. Today's ever-present markets have their own implicit values, and they can easily overwhelm whatever values leaders want to instill in their organizations.

Markets value what is exchangeable. They quantify value and measure it by price. In markets, human interactions are often transactions defined by who gets what. And markets tend to reduce human motivation to compensation by rewarding what pays. At bottom, the market perspective is highly individualistic, which makes it deeply antithetical to the whole notion of organizational values. It says to individuals: you are on your own and you better make the best deal you can for yourself. In the words of Robert Nozick, the libertarian philosopher, market-intensive capitalism is essentially a system of "capitalist acts between consenting adults."[1]

The tempting option for leaders today is to abandon the idea that the values inside their organizations can be very different from the values outside it and rely instead on market-based incentives, measures, and monitoring for achieving their organization's goals. This temptation is strong because the alternative of resisting the implicit values of markets can feel out of step with the times. Today, the pressure to make your numbers is transmitted, like a jolt of electricity, down and throughout organizations. And everyone in companies knows or should know they can be replaced, because the era of loyalty to employees is over, and deep, sophisticated labor markets make almost everyone fungible. This raises disturbing questions that can preoccupy managers. Where will they get their next job? Will it be a step up or down? And will they have the energy and drive to start climbing the greasy pole once again? Market values seem irresistible.

The alternative, which is hard and even daunting for leaders, is to take market pressures very seriously and respond to them in one of three basic ways. In some cases, responsible leaders actually try to intensify and accelerate market pressures. In other cases, they try to create organizational values that blunt or block market pressures, and, in still other situations, they commit themselves to values that transcend market forces.

To succeed in this effort, leaders need to do more than follow the standard, twentieth-century approach to values, which typically takes the form of lengthy lists of basic ethical principles and sound business values. Creating the right core values today involves focusing on another, much shorter set of values—clarity, meaningful projects, and bright ethical lines—that respond directly to the pressures, opportunities, and hazards of a recombinant world. A focus on clarity is a valuable way to accelerate market values. Meaningful projects are a critical way of transcending these pressures, and bright ethical lines can be crucial to blocking market pressures and reducing the risk of unethical, illegal, and damaging behavior in fluid, complex organizations.

To see why these three core values matter now, it is important to understand the role values played in classic twentieth-century organizations, see how they evolved into the contemporary litanies of consensus values, and understand the fading relevance of this approach. Against this background, the emerging approach to values—with its focus on clarity, meaningful projects, and bright ethical lines—stands out in sharp relief.

Cathedrals and Architects

An old story describes a traveler who talks with three stonecutters on a worksite in an English town. The traveler asks each what he is doing. The first says, "I'm earning a living." The second says, "I'm crafting a stone that will fit perfectly into that wall and make it strong." And the third stonecutter says, "I am helping Sir Christopher Wren build a magnificent cathedral to show the glory of God."

This story encapsulates the twentieth-century view of organizational values and its implications for leaders. The basic idea is that the world is divided into two categories: visionary leaders and their followers. True leaders, like Sir Christopher, think boldly and grandly, and they communicate their vision and values so powerfully that they give meaning and purpose to many others, like the third stonecutter.

For example, James Selznick, an important twentieth-century organizational thinker, argued that true leaders articulated a set of values and "institutionalized" them. This meant the values were woven into everyday life and routine decisions inside an organization. Selznick's perspective described the towering management role models of the last century. After Konosuke Matsushita died, Panasonic continued to operate by his principles, as did IBM after Thomas Watson, Sr., and General Motors after Alfred Sloan. Another important thinker, the historian and political scientist James MacGregor Burns, developed a more complex view of leadership, but, like Selznick, Burns put visionary leaders in a special category. In his classic work *Leadership*, published in 1978, Burns argued that the vast majority of managers were what he called transactional leaders, while a tiny handful were transformational.

Transactional leaders motivated other people and got work done with targets, monitoring, incentives, and reporting. They understood their roles and responsibilities within the larger structures around them. They planned, monitored, and executed. Like the second stonecutter, transactional leaders carefully fit each stone in place.

These men and women were usually called managers, not leaders. In contrast, transformational leaders motivated others through values and even reshaped their followers' values.

Like Selznick, Burns seemed to have described the great businesses of the twentieth century. At the top of these firms were the industrial statesmen—bold, forceful leaders, often the company founder, who had compelling visions about their businesses and, in many cases, about society as a whole, that they communicated to the ranks of salaried managers in their companies. Americans called these managers organization men; in Japan, they were salarymen; in Germany, *bueroangestellter*. The leader/manager distinction even seemed to hold outside the business world. In the middle of the last century, world-striding individuals such as Franklin D. Roosevelt, Mao Zedong, and Winston Churchill inspired and reshaped societies by leading vast military and political hierarchies staffed by millions of nameless soldiers and civil servants and run day by day through several levels of "middle management."

Burns and Selznick also provided a fresh and powerful perspective on the great industrial machines of the twentieth century. It was easy to think of these organizations as giant machines administered by soulless managers, with each manager assigned to a tiny cell in a vast structure of roles, responsibilities, and rules. Burns and Selznick understood that large organizations were also human communities and could be suffused with value and purpose. Their view of large organizations gave responsible leaders a clear mandate: instilling a sense of meaning into what would otherwise be mechanistic structures that reduced humans to automatons. True leaders would help other members of an organization feel like the third stonecutter and believe they were contributing to larger, abiding aims.

The Crisis of "Cathedral" Values

Despite its power, the classic model of inspiring leaders and inspired followers was seriously flawed. Like stonecutting, work in the giant manufacturing operations of the twentieth century was often boring, repetitive, hard, and at times dangerous. And office work, while safer, could be dull and dehumanizing: the "organization man" was a target of criticism, not a role model.[2] In other words, a vaguely religious superstructure of purpose, mission, credo, and social contribution didn't change many of the hard facts of organization life. And the harsher critics of industrial capitalism viewed the noble rhetoric of transformational leadership as an exceedingly clever way of concealing, protecting, and legitimating concentrated economic power and its frequent abuse.

In recent decades, some of the gaps in the traditional view of corporate leadership have widened into chasms. A widespread challenge is inculcating values when workers and staff change organizations frequently. Another factor is widespread cynicism about the real motives of business leaders. Scandals underscore this issue, as do the executives whose real commitments seem to be to their compensation packages—some of which are larger than the budgets of many towns—and not their corporate values.

Another problem was surprising: because senior executives began taking values more seriously, statements of corporate values became standardized and even stale. The problem worsened as companies became global, because values had to be phrased in very general terms to cover wide ranges of business, legal, and cultural practices. In the end, these statements became so broad that they seemed to have little real content and could justify a wide range of approaches to problems and opportunities.

These generic statements elicit skeptical and dismissive comments, even from the CEOs of major companies. The head of a major European energy firm, for example, said:

> *I read very often on the back of annual reports of companies the vision of the company, and I read many complicated things that seem to come from textbooks or consultants. They say the vision of the company is to so and so and so and improve customer satisfaction or whatever.*[3]

A recent study found striking similarities in the content and even the exact phrasing of many corporate mission statements and codes of ethics—as if they, like so much else today, had been modularized.[4]

As CEO of Microsoft, Bill Gates warned against broad, pseudovisionary pronouncements, dismissing them as

"MIPS to the moon" talk.[5] Lou Gerstner took a similar view when he became CEO of the near-bankrupt IBM and said that the last thing the company needed was a "vision."[6] These statements—from one of the most successful entrepreneurs of modern times and from a big-company executive who saved and transformed IBM—reinforce the serious questions about the "grand cathedral" view of mission and values.

Rethinking Responsibility

The main reason to rethink the classic approach to values is that it is better suited to traditional, institutional capitalism rather than contemporary, entrepreneurial capitalism. A great deal of leadership work today is highly transactional, as leaders shepherd evolving commitments through complexities, surprises, and turbulence. When companies are platforms for constant reconfiguration, leaders need finely honed negotiation skills. In always-on markets, leaders are constantly engaged in "deal making" of various kinds. In short, in a market-driven world, a great deal of important activity involves transactions and streams of transactions. These have to be guided, shaped, and structured appropriately, and this is the responsibility of leaders. In other words, leadership today is heavily "transactional." This isn't a diluted or second-best version of leadership: it is simply leadership.

The distinction between leaders and managers, which was always overdrawn, is now barely useful. It was based on looking at the world through a traditional lens, seeing a world of hierarchies, and concluding that responsible leadership involved inspirational leaders at the peaks of these hierarchies. This was inevitably a simplification, but it captured elements of truth. But a contemporary perspective highlights networks of always-shifting talent, ideas, technology, and chunks of organization, with leaders in the middle of almost continuous adjustment, negotiation, nudging, and readjustment.

This means the venerable leader/manager distinction now deserves a prominent display case in the museum of management thinking. Charismatic leaders haven't disappeared and never will, nor will bureaucrats, but neither term describes much of management reality today. Today, responsible leaders need alternatives to generic corporate statements for thinking about values. In particular, they need a way to think about values that reflects and capitalizes on the market forces pervading our world.

Consensus Values and Core Values

What is the alternative to the "grand cathedral and great architect" approach? What approach to organizational values has some prospect of surviving and transcending the pressures of intensely competitive markets and the implicit values these markets promote? The emerging answer may be that leaders should distinguish two different kinds of values—*consensus* values and *core* values—and pay vigilant attention to core values.

Consensus values are familiar because they reflect the grand cathedral view and have become a common corporate practice. They can be found in the value statements of many large companies, and they have three basic elements. One is some overarching statement. It typically says how the company will change the world and make some significant contribution to the society around it. The mission of Whole Foods, for example, is framed in terms of "whole foods, whole planet, whole people," and Apple wants to "put a dent in the universe." The second element is typically a list of basic values such as honesty, integrity, and respect for individuals, communities, and the law. The third element is often a statement of responsibilities to particular stakeholder groups.[7]

The consensus values are easy to criticize as vague, internally inconsistent, commonsensical, or hypocritical. But they reflect a deep need in human nature and serve as a counterweight to market values. As one entrepreneur put it, "Without chasing something important, timeless, truly differentiated in the marketplace, the forces that stall out virtually all business organizations will take hold. Without boldness of purpose, it is harder to succeed."[8]

Moreover, no one would want to live or work in a world where powerful institutions and their leaders failed to meet minimum standards of ethics, responsibility, and civility. The consensus values may look obvious to observers sitting in the grandstands, but experienced leaders understand how hard it is—in the face of grueling competition, ubiquitous complexity in which scoundrels can hide, and strong pressures to do as the Romans do—to ensure that their organizations reliably meet the consensus values. In short, consensus values matter, even if they often elicit indifference, skepticism, and even cynicism.

But core values *really* matter. These are the values a leader, a senior management team, and an organization will struggle, long and hard, to make good on. Typically, these values elicit intense commitment because they reinforce a company's strategy and because its leader is deeply and personally committed to them.

In other words, responsible leaders are jugglers. Consensus values are balls that they try hard not to drop. Core values are balls that they believe must absolutely stay in the air. As such, the acid test of a core value is neither words nor deeds. It is willingness to struggle long and hard—with courage, imagination, and steely tenacity—to make good on a commitment to that value.

Virtually all organizations have core values, but they often remain implicit, concealed behind broad-brush mission statements that commit organizations to almost everything. But most people who have worked in an organization for a while learn what its core values really are. They learn this by seeing what leaders do when hard choices have to be made, because these choices reveal what leaders really value. Core values elicit long nights, grueling effort, real trepidation about failure, and widespread elation at success.

Generalizations are hazardous, but the experience of entrepreneurs indicates that a strong personal commitment to three core values is essential to responsible, successful leadership today. These core values are clarity, meaningful projects, and bright ethical lines. In different ways, each of these helps leaders and organizations respond to the risks and opportunities created by pervasive market forces.

Clarity

A century ago, Supreme Court Justice Louis Brandeis wrote a famous endorsement of transparency: "Sunshine is said to be the best disinfectant."[9] He said this at a time when giant industrial firms were appearing throughout the economy and it was much harder for outsiders to understand what was happening inside them. During their heyday, these firms had huge cash flows, and executives were naturally tempted to play a variety of games with information—to advance their careers, firm up relationships with legislators and regulators, support pet projects, and advance their protégés. In some companies, these games became a minor art form. Transparency helped mitigate this problem, in large firms and other large institutions throughout society.

Transparency still matters today, but when competition is intense, organizations are fragile, success depends heavily on innovation, and plans are deeply fallible, leaders need to go one step further and commit themselves and their organizations to clarity. This means, in practice, that leaders take the initiative and say to other parties—in direct, straightforward ways—"Here is what you need to know," "This is what is going well and what really isn't," or "This is the big problem we need to fix."

Christopher Michel, the managing director of Nautilus Ventures and founder of Affinity Labs—which builds specialized social networks for firefighters, nurses, and other groups—defined clarity this way:

> *It is conveying what is important in an objective way . . . It is unblinking, unvarnished presentations and being totally clear when there is an elephant in the room. It is a commitment that everyone understand just what the issue is. It is completely acknowledging the situation and providing clarity about it, about key facts, and about hard issues and conflicts. Some people have an artful way of bringing up hard issues and conflicts, and some don't, but you have to bring them up.*[10]

Why is a core commitment to clarity so valuable today? The basic reason is that clarity exploits the inevitable: it is a way to take the inescapable market pressures for up-to-date information and shape them in ways that can help an organization survive and even thrive.

Markets are extraordinarily useful communication devices. At the simplest level, they inform buyers and sellers about prices. But many markets today communicate far more, because they are based on so-called relational contracts.[11] This means the parties work together, sometimes over years, and get to know a good deal about each other. As a result, clarity, almost inevitably, elicits reactions—often, informed and valuable reactions—from these other parties. This enables them to communicate about the standards that a leader and an organization have to meet to continue or improve a relationship and about changes that need to be made.

This is particularly true in times of turbulence. In the face of deep uncertainty and complexity, no leader and no organization, however brilliant, can do it alone. They need to be engaged in a dialogue with other parties about what they need to accomplish and do. Put differently, candor and accountability create a valuable, practical conversation for leaders and organizations, and this is particularly true in today's multimarket world.

Google chose this option during a heated public controversy about censorship in China and the alleged complicity of companies such as Yahoo!, Cisco, and Google—all dedicated to the free flow of information—with what has been called "the great firewall of China." A public statement from Google said:

> *Self-censorship, like that which we are now required to perform in China, is something that conflicts deeply with our core principles. We recognize the conflict and the inconsistency . . . It is not appropriate to say that we are proud of our decision. It is just too early to say that. Our hope is that the decision will prove to be the right one. If, over time, we are not able to achieve our objectives to continue to balance those interests in China, we will not hesitate to reconsider doing business in that market.*[12]

Candid communication like this often elicits strong reaction, recommendations, incentives, and pressures, because ubiquitous markets give investors, customers, talent, partners, and government bodies other options. The external parties say, in effect, "Get to work on these problems and make some progress, or explain to us why you're not, because otherwise we will look for other opportunities." This can be uncomfortable or painful in the short run, but a strong bias toward clarity can help leaders hear analysis and recommendations that they need to hear—and hear them sooner rather than later.[13]

Clarity also pays valuable dividends inside an organization. Many organizations today are platforms, face intense competition, and are competing on knowledge and information. This makes it critical for information to move rapidly within an organization. And moving rapidly means moving laterally—across departments, units, divisions, teams, and task forces—rather than up and down a classic hierarchy. Clarity also makes it easier for leaders and others to understand what is going on in organizations and in markets that are full of complex, unpredictable interactions among a wide, ever-shifting range of people, technologies, partnerships, experiments, and surprises.

All this may sound sensible, but leaders facing intense performance pressure require intellectual, psychological, and emotional courage to follow facts and analysis as far as possible and to disclose what they find. Sometimes an honest examination of the facts reveals no clear answers or reveals that past answers that are now being translated into detailed plans and actions need reconsideration. A natural tendency is to look away from this analysis, just as people sometimes avoid doctors because they don't want to hear a particular recommendation.

The struggle for clarity often means focusing on the realities of risks and problems. This is hard for many leaders. They are typically men and women with abundant confidence, optimism, and strong faith in themselves, their work, and the people around them. They also know that negative sentiments from a leader can spread like a contagion. And when so much of the future is blank space, the temptation is to look away from the prospect of failure and fill one's imagination and the airwaves with upbeat statements. Another unfortunate option is to play some of the conventional games that many large, established companies have transformed into art forms— dissembling news releases, minimal compliance with government disclosure requirements, relentlessly optimistic interpretations of uncertain situations, keeping information from boards, and diverting regulators' attention from real problems.

It takes intellectual and moral strength for leader to put up a big sign saying, "We just don't know, despite our best efforts," or a sign saying, "Here's what we know, and it's complicated, and we have to keep working and be flexible, and see what we learn," or "I'm afraid we've been going down the wrong path." This is why clarity is essentially self-administered medicine. It tastes bad, but the treatment is usually a better option than ignoring symptoms and delaying the inevitable.

Most entrepreneurs know, all too well, that problems, surprises, and failures, large and small, are facts of life. In fact, the bolder the innovation and ambition, the more likely they are. In recent years, various groups have tried to destigmatize failure and its disclosure for entrepreneurs in the private and nonprofit sectors. For example, the World Bank held an international FAILFaire in 2012 to help participants understand that failure was an inescapable part of innovative development work. A major theme at the event was the importance of finding donors who did not expect to be continuously dazzled but understood the vulnerability of the projects they supported and could help organizations deal with mishaps.[14]

What does clarity mean in practice? Above all, it means that a leader consistently demonstrates a strong bias toward candor, disclosure, and openness. It means answering the question that is actually being asked, even if it is awkward, rather than diverting the conversation and hoping that others will not challenge the leader's authority and raise the awkward topic again. Leaders who are committed to clarity don't play games with information and discourage others from doing so, readily admit errors and uncertainties, praise and reward candor in others, and push hard for realistic, fact-based assessments of situations and problems.

As with any serious commitment, the acid test of clarity is daily behavior—not just by a leader, but throughout an organization. The basic question is how many meetings, watercooler conversations, and e-mail exchanges have statements to the effect of "Here is what you really need to know," "This is what we really have to talk about," or "Here is what's driving me crazy." In short, in an organization committed to clarity, the elephants in the room are rarely ignored.

One of the best-known examples of corporate clarity was Johnson & Johnson's response to the deaths of seven people in the Chicago area who had taken cyanide-laced Tylenol. The company decided immediately that it would disclose everything it knew to the media, government agencies, and local communities. In return, J&J hoped it would gain information or insights that could help it understand what had happened. The company persisted with this policy despite serious bumps in the road. At one point, for example, J&J said that there was cyanide in the plant that made the poisoned capsules. Later, it had to correct that statement, in public, because it learned that small amounts of cyanide were used in the plant's quality control process. After the crisis ended, J&J was widely praised for its candor, and its crisis management response became a model for other organizations.

Unfortunately, in recent years, J&J has failed to follow its own example. Between 2009 and 2012, the company had a seemingly endless series of product problems. It tried to conceal some of them, made partial disclosures in other cases, and created widespread skepticism and cynicism about its operations and the trustworthiness of its leaders. In fact, the persistent avoidance of accountability through candor may have ultimately cost the CEO his job.

Where should leaders and organizations draw the line between clarity about important information, serious problems, and valuable opportunities on the one hand and the responsible management or even concealment of strategic or confidential information on the other? There is no simple answer to this question, but one entrepreneur suggested a useful guideline. Janet Kraus, the cofounder of Circles, a large concierge and events organizer, said she tried to put herself in the shoes of the other party—which could be an investor, a customer, an employee, or a government regulator—and then ask if she would feel she had legitimate grounds for requesting and getting a particular piece of information. If the answer was no, the conversation should probably move to other topics. If the answer was yes, the information should probably be disclosed, and a leader and an organization needed to pay close attention to what they then heard.[15]

This test provides only a minimum standard for candor. It indicates what should be disclosed, given the legitimate interests and rights of another party. A broader standard asks what a leader and an organization can learn from disclosing information and paying close attention to the reactions of knowledgeable, committed parties. Both standards—the legitimacy test and the learning test—are ways of countering the almost endless series of excuses for blocking the flow of information into markets: the possibility it could be used against an organization in court, the risk that the press will misinterpret it, or the handy caricature of financial markets as hair-trigger, short term, and fad driven. In fact, several recent, large-scale, quantitative studies strongly suggest that transparency with financial markets can create a forum for valuable two-way dialogue between investors and company leaders.[16]

The old saying "Best friends only tell their best friends" encapsulates a good deal of practical wisdom. Today's intensely competitive, always-on markets are voracious consumers of knowledge, data, rumors, and all sorts of bits and scraps of information. The blurry boundaries around organizations today are leaky boundaries. As a result, leaders need to be realistic and realize that, in many cases, they cannot avoid the intense market pressure for transparency. All they can really do is choose between better and worse versions of it. The inferior version is clarity that comes late, reluctantly, and partially, and stokes whatever suspicions external parties had initially. The superior form of clarity is clear, timely, and full, and enhances the trust and credibility people place in an organization and its leaders.

Meaningful Projects

Clarity is a valuable way of taking advantage of market forces, but responsible leadership today often requires a second core commitment: to transcending market forces by creating, nurturing, and protecting meaningful projects.

In an intensely competitive world, survival and success depend crucially on the tenacity, creativity, and passion of leaders and many others in an organization, but deep commitment isn't a commodity traded in markets. People commit and struggle hard because an activity or a goal really means something to them. The great industrial statesmen understood this, and so do most entrepreneurs. But where does meaning come from when so much is uncertain, temporary, and fallible?

In a recent confidential conversation, a very successful biotech entrepreneur and investor made a provocative and intriguing statement. "Nobody," she said, "wants a detailed credo. They want a lot of space for personal initiative and a project that inspires them personally. In one company I know, everyone is excited about creating what they call 'surgery without a knife.' It isn't just about pay because, for the top people, pay is available elsewhere. It's about what the project means to them."

This statement is provocative because it suggests that talented people now put little stock in traditional corporate credos and mission statements. In other words, in a fluid, market-driven economy, employees are much less likely to see themselves as career stonemasons at work on giant, permanent edifices. Entrepreneurs do pursue grand visions and ambitions, and a tiny handful succeed, but they also understand, in their bones, the favorite phrase of Ed Zschau, a successful entrepreneur and venture capitalist who now teaches in the engineering department at Princeton: "Nothing is forever."[17]

A new company could, of course, become another IBM and last a century, but today's stunning success is often tomorrow's also-ran, acquisition, or failure. In this respect, the biotech entrepreneur's statement simply reflects the realities of the new invisible hand. Moreover, her view is consistent with recent research on how to motivate talented individuals. For example, a recent *Harvard Business Review* article on managing creative people made no mention of credos or corporate mission statements.[18]

But these developments make the entrepreneur's statement intriguing. She refers to excitement, initiative, and inspiration. Where do these come from when jobs, career plans, and entire organizations can vanish on short notice? Why do so many people work so intensely in entrepreneurial organizations if they don't have the sense they are building something likely to endure?

The answer lies, at least in part, in a second core value of responsible leaders. They are deeply committed to creating, understanding in depth, and personally supporting a wide range of meaningful projects in their organizations. These leaders and their companies may also adopt some version of the standardized consensus-value credos and mission statements, because these are nearly obligatory today, and they typically offer financial rewards for success. But their organizations achieve white-hot focus and intensity because, day by day and week by week, people in the organization feel they are working on projects that really matter.

"Surgery without a knife" is a metaphor for tasks that elicit intense commitment because the people working on them feel they can have a clear, direct, immediate or near-term impact. They feel they are close to doing something important—for a customer, a client, or a community—and for their company. Put differently, meaning and value come from creating the contemporary equivalent of a gargoyle or a beautiful piece of stained glass, not from adding another stone to a grand, enduring edifice.

Long-term vision is widely encouraged and praised, but it can easily ring hollow. An intense effort to create something like "surgery without a knife" might produce a dramatic breakthrough that changes medicine, creates an important new healthcare company, and showers wealth on its founders, early investors, and employees. But in a fluid, knowledge-driven world, the far more likely scenario is that many firms, along with universities and consortia of various kinds, are working on similar projects. At some unknown future point, some of these efforts might somehow converge and slowly begin to change what surgeons and hospitals do. But all these prospects are distant, speculative, and highly uncertain.

Compelling value and meaning have to come from the shorter-term impact of a project and the challenges it poses—conceptual, technological, and managerial—for the people on a project team. Entrepreneurial organizations illustrate this point clearly because most of them are essentially a single, large, all-eggs-in-the-basket project. But many large firms are now reshaping themselves into networks of knowledge-based, specialized activity in which the project is the basic unit of activity.

The importance of shorter-term "micro" goals rather than long-range "macro" goals was revealed in a large, rigorous, multiyear study of the daily experiences of teams in eight companies. The study demonstrated the importance of the inner lives of employees to the success of their work and, in turn, the importance of efforts by senior managers to enable employees and teams to make progress on tasks and projects. What proved valuable wasn't leaders' sweeping, inspiring references to a long-term company vision. It was their small, everyday gestures and efforts that affirmed the values of projects and cleared a path for their success by providing clear goals, resources, autonomy, and sound, honest feedback.[19]

In practical terms, leaders with a strong project focus help people in their organizations answer three questions: Am I making a real contribution to an exciting and potentially important project? Do I have the chance to take initiative and put my stamp on some aspect of the project? And, if we succeed, will I get the reward I deserve, in compensation and in new opportunities?

For leaders, this is a very demanding challenge. It involves a constant struggle against quick-fix, short-term solutions. It demands that leaders really understand the units, task forces, and groups in an organization, so they can say—in detail and convincingly—why their efforts really matter. All in all, a core commitment to meaningful projects makes for even longer days for already overscheduled leaders.

The struggle to create a widespread project mentality matters for two reasons. First, it can determine survival and success. Intense commitment enables organizations to move fast, adapt quickly, sweat the small details so often critical to success, squeeze as much value as possible out of limited resources, and scour their environments for opportunities. In a recombinant world in which so much is readily copyable, the intensity, spirit, and drive of an organization can be decisive for success.

In the end, of course, a company's projects must reinforce each other in ways that help it pursue, adjust, and succeed in meeting its commitments in all its markets. Some projects will succeed brilliantly and others will fail; some failures may be experiments that teach valuable lessons, and some may make little more than solid contributions to a company's longer-term aims. But in a market-driven world in which many breakthroughs are basically impermanent and quickly replicated elsewhere, success often depends not just on the constellation of projects in a company but on the intensity that teams and their leaders devote to these projects.

The challenge of creating, understanding, and supporting meaningful projects also matters because the men and women who create successful organizations are doing more than providing jobs, income, and some degree of security for employees and those who depend on them. They are also providing islands of purpose and meaning. This is a genuine and important contribution to others' lives, particularly in economies and societies that often feel fractured and fluid.

Vigilance about Bright Lines

Markets create enormous pressures for successful performance and sometimes reward it spectacularly. This puts leaders and others under enormous pressure to take actions that achieve market metrics but may be short-sighted. Even worse, when intense competitive pressure says "Make your numbers or else," people can feel strong pressure to play games, bend rules, break the law, or violate ethical standards. The pressures are very strong. Good people can succumb to them, and weak or corrupt employees can decide to grab some of the goodies while they can. If a company competes internationally, much can be rationalized on a "lowest common denominator" global standard.

Because of all these risks, the third core value of responsible leaders today is a commitment to clear bright lines as ways of blocking dangerous market pressures. For example, Warren Buffett became CEO of Salomon Brothers in 1991 because repeated ethical violations had brought the firm to the brink of collapse. A trader had repeatedly broken Treasury Department rules, and the previous CEO had covered this up. Salomon urgently needed Buffett's financial backing, credibility, and reputation for integrity. As an investment bank, Salomon Brothers depended critically on short-term credit from other banks, and this, in turn, depended on their trust and confidence in Salomon Brothers. One of Buffett's first statements, broadcast to all the bank's employees, was succinct, blunt, and personal. "If you lose money for the firm by bad decisions," he said, "I will be very understanding. If you lose reputation, I will be ruthless."[20]

Buffett made a personal commitment to clear bright lines. These are values that a leader believes are so important that, when employees violate them, they are fired or find themselves on very strict probation. Values are typically described in broad, general, flexible terms, so why do some of them need to be stated in sharp, almost draconian terms and reinforced by explicit, personal commitment from an organization's leaders? There are three strong reasons why some values need to be treated as bright lines.

First, as we have seen, the new invisible hand is a world of complex, fluid organizations surrounded by shifting networks of complex relationships. This creates myriad opportunities for people to commit wrongdoing and hide it. Innovative activities provide even more opportunities for mischief making and worse because control systems, norms, and ethical principles often lag behind innovations or don't seem to apply to them. Finally, the temptation to exploit these opportunities is especially strong in a market-driven world because performance pressures are intense, no job is guaranteed, and success, real or fake, can lead to outsized rewards.

All these risks grow greater because there are some people for whom ethics is simply a calculation. Before they decide whether to do what is right, they do a quick cost-benefit analysis. They compare the option of doing what is wrong—its costs, benefits, and risks—with the option of doing the right thing. And as the world grows more complex, the chances of getting caught seem to fall and doing what is wrong becomes more attractive. This is why Buffett's example and his threat to be "ruthless" are sadly but powerfully realistic.

The second reason for bright-line values is that a connected, multimarket world is a "trip wire" world. One mistake or one illegal act, even by an obscure middle manager, can ripple through the markets around an organization and damage it badly. The most memorable example of a trip wire calamity involved a young banker in the Singapore office of Baring Brothers, a global investment bank. He had the authority to trade for the firm and was also responsible for settling accounts at the end of each day. This dual role enabled him to make a secret $1 billion bet on the Japanese stock market. Shortly afterward, the Kobe earthquake led to a dramatic drop in share prices, and the entire equity of Baring Brothers, a sum accumulated over two centuries, was wiped out; the firm soon disappeared.

If a giant firm such as Baring Brothers can be destroyed by a trip wire hazard, smaller organizations are even more vulnerable. One entrepreneur, speaking confidentially, believed he had addressed this risk with a bright line encapsulated in a single word: lying. This was his way of addressing a legal and ethical problem that is particularly acute for innovative organizations. The problem has many colorful names—such as boosterism, puffery, and brochuremanship—but they all involve the question of how far to stretch the truth. This can be a tricky question, but the entrepreneur took a hard line. "Some boosterism is just lying," he said. "It is misstating plain, obvious, certain facts, or making up facts out of thin air. I don't tolerate that."

In another confidential interview, a widely known entrepreneur drew a similar line. "You actually don't know the odds the business will succeed or our product will perform as expected. You just know that the odds are low. You can paint the future, but the key thing is that the future you paint should not be one you know is wrong." Both these entrepreneurs believed that lying was wrong on basic ethical terms. They also knew that word spreads quickly through the networks of relationships surrounding companies today and can quickly damage the reputation of a company and its leader. When suspicion spreads, markets basically follow an old Italian saying that advises, "Believe none of what you hear and half of what you see." These suspicions can seriously handicap a company in all the markets it depends on.

The third reason for bright-line values is simple, and Warren Buffett made it clear in the Salomon Brothers situation. CEOs often draw bright lines because of their own personal ethical convictions and because they see their companies as extensions of themselves. This is often the case in entrepreneurial companies, where the founder treats the firm as his or her "baby."

These leaders also understand that a white-hot dedication to an organization's success can lead good people to take shortcuts or break the rules out of intense but misguided commitment. In short, when leaders succeed in creating intensely committed teams focused on critical projects and motivated by a wide range of deep feelings, values, and interests, they are playing with fire. They have created the organizational equivalent of a blowtorch—a powerful tool that has to be handled with extreme care.

Credibility is the hard practical challenge for leaders who want to draw bright lines. Saying the right thing—about reputation or lying, for example—is easy, but making a leader's commitment clear is difficult. Surprisingly, a valuable guideline for creating credibility was put in a memorable phrase by an individual who struggled hard to break through barriers but was hardly a conventional entrepreneur. His name, before he became famous as Muhammad Ali, was Cassius Clay. He was an extraordinarily quick and intelligent boxer, but he lacked the size and strength of many of his opponents. Before a fight with Sonny Liston, the reigning world heavyweight champion and a powerful, tough fighter, the twenty-two-year-old Clay said he would "float like a butterfly and sting like a bee." Once the fight started, Liston exhausted himself trying to hit his elusive opponent. Clay eventually landed several well-timed, punishing blows, and won the bout in seven rounds.[21]

"Stinging like a bee" means that a leader imposes real costs on people who cross bright lines, and these costs are what create credibility. This happens when a leader penalizes or fires a star performer for crossing a bright line.

It happens when a company says no to a lucrative deal with a customer if the relationship would violate a bright line. It happens when a company says no to attractive financing if it would create pressure to violate company values. Leaders "float like a butterfly" by looking vigilantly, closely, and continuously for violations of basic values. When they see a problem, they act decisively and "sting like a bee."

Bright lines shouldn't be crossed, and they shouldn't be approached. When this is widely understood, bright lines provide a valuable early-warning system that can help organizations avert problems and even disasters. Preet Bharara, the US Attorney for the Southern District of New York, explained this in simple, blunt terms. "If you are single-mindedly focused on walking the line, you are bound to end up afoul of regulators, and God forbid, criminal prosecutors," he said. "Even more dangerous perhaps, you are sending a message to every other person at the firm that line-walking is a good idea. That can work for a while, but people will invariably miscalculate and bad things will invariably follow."[22]

Bright-line values shouldn't be viewed as crude behavior modification through threats and fear—in other words, as contemporary versions of hanging thieves for minor offenses. Responsible leaders have two messages about bright-line values. One is a warning not to violate them or risk doing so. The other says, in effect, "If you think you're close to crossing one of these bright, red lines, surface the issue and let others help you resolve it."

Responsible leaders praise, assist, and reward the people who step forward and highlight risky situations, and they counsel and sometimes penalize those who don't.

Struggle and Courage

Each of the three core commitments—to clarity, meaningful projects, and vigilance about bright lines—requires leaders to struggle, sometimes courageously. In part, the struggle reflects the pressures and temptations of a market-driven world. Competitive pressures lead to an intense focus on profits and the task at hand, rather than longer-term, intangible considerations such as values. Employees who move in and out of organizations, in the always-on market for talent, have less time and sometimes less incentive to learn, really understand, and personally commit to the core values or consensus values. Moreover, employees in organizations that operate in several countries are influenced, consciously and unconsciously, by a wide range of values and practices, and these can run counter to an organization's values.

Moreover, two of the three core values lead to distinctive struggles. Clarity invites market judgments that can be painful for leaders and organizations, especially if things aren't going well. It takes commitment and courage for a leader to avoid the standard diversionary tactics and instead disclose difficult or awkward information and let other parties hold the leader and an organization accountable.

A genuine commitment to bright lines takes courage because of the costs that make this commitment credible. If a leader fires "good old Pete" for crossing a bright line, and everyone knows that Pete was already on his way out, the result is simply cynicism about bright lines and a clear sense that the leader views them as a handy tactic and not a serious personal commitment. But the price for taking action when a star performer or an important client crosses a bright line can be high. These costs can be viewed as an investment whose payoff is fewer violations in the future, but their short-term impact is a test—often a public, closely watched test—of whether a leader actually has the courage to stand behind his or her commitments.

Cumulative Demands of Leadership Today

This chapter and the three before it sketched emerging answers to the enduring questions of responsible leadership. They did this by describing a range of important commitments and the struggles these commitments entail. Almost inevitably, the men and women who try to lead responsibly in an entrepreneurial world will sometimes find themselves asking whether the struggle is worth it. When they ask this question, they are raising the last of the enduring questions of responsible leadership.

One answer is that positions of leadership, despite their demands, offer pay and perks, status and power, and the possibility of success, renown, and perhaps even wealth. But this rationale relies on a self-interested calculation of costs and benefits. It means that, when the costs and risks out-weigh the benefits, leaders will cut back their efforts, rene-gotiate their pay packages, or fold up their tents and move on. But true leaders—the heroic ones we know and the quiet ones who matter so much in every organization—aren't continuously calculating the present value of their efforts. They work and struggle courageously because they are pursuing something much deeper. The next chapter explains what drives them onward.

CHAPTER SIX

WHY HAVE I CHOSEN THIS LIFE?

The final enduring question of responsible leadership seems radically different from the first one, yet the two are closely connected. The first question asks leaders to look at the world around them and make sure they are working hard to grasp the fundamentals. In contrast, the last enduring question asks leaders to step back and ask, Why have I chosen this life? What aims and ideals am I pursuing?

These two questions are entwined because fundamental forces in the world today, particularly market-driven recombination, can make leadership an especially demanding struggle. As a result, responsible leaders—at all levels of organizations—will sometimes ask whether their hard work and sacrifice are really worth it. They can feel like Sisyphus, the ancient Greek king condemned by the gods to push a heavy rock to the top of a steep hill, only to see it roll back to the bottom, again and again, for all eternity.

To some extent, moments of serious misgivings are unavoidable. If we put aside romanticized accounts, we find that leadership has always been a struggle—to set and communicate the right goals, succeed against competitors, fight internal political battles, balance competing pressures and obligations, and maintain personal discipline, confidence, and focus. But these inescapable challenges of leadership are all intensified today, and each of the emerging answers to the enduring questions reflects this.

In a fluid, recombinant world, competition is relentless and uncertainty runs high. Leaders face continuous performance pressures in the markets for customers, funds, talent, capabilities, partners, government influence, and meaning. Traditional decision making and planning are much less reliable. Organizations have to be efficient and focused, even though they are immersed in complex, fluid networks of hard-to-manage relationships. Organizational values are hard to communicate with so much change, skepticism, and short-term performance pressure.

Given all these challenges, it is no surprise that leaders can feel stranded, particularly if boards of directors, existing regulations, and familiar industry norms provide only limited guidance on the new and complex issues arising from innovation and complex recombination. Leaders who take their responsibility seriously can easily find themselves in the kind of predicament described by Daniel Callahan, a pioneer in medical ethics, when he wrote, "I learned right from wrong at my mother's knee, but she didn't teach me about the ethics of fetal organ transplants."[1]

On top of all these challenges, leaders also have to deal with the everyday physical struggle of their work. To outsiders, leadership can look like an orderly, safe, quiet activity performed in well-appointed offices. The reality is that a leader's workday often begins in morning darkness, and meetings can run past dinnertime. A normal week can include several plane flights, and the last workday in the week is often Sunday, a traditional day of rest. In addition, leaders who understand their responsibilities and the consequences their decisions have for other people carry a heavier burden because they know and feel the full human impact of failure.

So it is almost inevitable that leaders will sometimes ask themselves, Why am I taking on this struggle? On some days, the answer is "Because it's part of something larger that is exciting, important, or making the world a better place." On other days, the answer is very pragmatic—some version of "This is what I'm paid for" or " It's how I put bread on the table" or "That is why it's called work."

This book puts a sharp edge on the last enduring question. It defines responsible leadership today as a long struggle, demanding perseverance and courage, to make good on serious but fallible commitments in an uncertain and unforgiving world. This can easily sound like the labor of Sisyphus. Perhaps a much better approach is to focus on the confidence and optimism that motivates leaders and the exciting entrepreneurial opportunities created by the new invisible hand. Unfortunately, this beguiling approach is just a diversion from hard, almost inescapable questions about leadership and life.

The last enduring question reflects themes that run through ancient wisdom, almost every religious and philosophical tradition, and most classic literature. One theme is that leadership is hard because life is hard. The Book of Job tells us, "Man, born of woman, scant of days, and sated with trouble, like a blossom he comes forth and withers, and flees like a shadow—he will not stay."[2] Another longstanding view says that if life is hard, leadership is even harder. Niccolò Machiavelli, a close student of history and classic philosophy, used a familiar image to describe the precarious position that leaders occupy. He compared fortune to a great river that often flows calmly, but sometimes rages without warning and sweeps everything away. After surveying history from the ancient Greeks through the Renaissance, Machiavelli concluded that, "There is nothing more dangerous than the creation of a new order of things."[3]

Yet another longstanding theme is that leadership is hard not just because the world is hazardous, but because leaders are human and therefore flawed, vulnerable, and prone to illusion and error. For example, Shakespeare writes in *Macbeth*,

> *O, but man, proud man! Dress'd in a little brief authority;*
> *Most ignorant of what he's most assur'd,*
> *His glassy essence, like an angry ape,*
> *Plays such fantastic tricks before high heaven,*
> *As make the angels weep.*

In short, what can look like a pessimistic view of leadership may actually be realism, and the final enduring question asks leaders to reflect seriously, from time to time, on this perspective on their work. Even in the large, stable hierarchies of the twentieth century, the hard, personal challenges of leadership were inescapable, and it is important to understand how leaders in these organizations addressed this daunting personal challenge so we can see what is distinctive and important about the answer emerging today.

My Station and Its Duties

Perhaps the most vivid description of leadership and struggle in classic, hierarchical organizations came from a remarkable individual named Chester Barnard. He had the talent to become a successful AT&T executive during the 1920s, when Ma Bell was an exciting, fast-growing, high-tech company, and he also had the mind of a first-rate academic theorist. Barnard distilled what he learned from running a large, complicated organization into a book, *The Functions of the Executive*, that is one of the last century's classic conceptual works on leadership and organizations. Barnard describes the challenge of leadership this way: "It seems to me inevitable that the struggle to create cooperation among men should as surely destroy some men morally as battle destroys them physically."[4]

These are very strong words. So why did the executives who ran the classic hierarchical firms persist in hard struggles that Barnard compared to physical combat? The basic answer was that organizational roles helped them understand what they were supposed to do and, more important, why it really mattered. By leading an organization or their part of one, these managers were contributing to its larger purpose. Moreover, they weren't alone. Other leaders, managing other parts of the organization, were also part of the same concerted effort—focused and disciplined by hierarchy and aiming at some larger, fundamental goals.

This way of justifying the struggle of leadership was particularly effective in companies led by the great industrial statesmen. They articulated the larger social and economic roles of their firms and explained, in compelling ways, how individual efforts served larger purposes. In Japan and Germany, during the postwar years, the grand cause was rebuilding a country and restoring its pride. At other times and places, the larger cause was creating new industries, jobs, and wealth. The statement "What's good for GM is good for the country, and vice versa" may now sound antiquated, but it sketched an important role in society for GM managers—a role confirmed by GM's extraordinary contributions to the war effort and its central role, over many decades, in the US economy. All this helped justify leaders' struggles.[5]

At the same time, their struggle was often less challenging than today because competition was less intense and business was less risky and uncertain. Many of the successful, dominant firms of the last half-century were oligopolies. They competed primarily in national markets. Friendly government regulation often limited competition even further. With quasi-lifetime employment, managers and leaders did not feel their jobs were permanently at risk. In some large, well-established companies, the most intense struggle for senior executives was the internal political battle to become CEO, not the external battle with competitors.

But the twentieth-century institutional setting didn't shield managers from personal questions about whether their efforts really mattered. Some of the most compelling literature of the midcentury—such as *Death of a Salesman* by Arthur Miller and *The Organization Man* by William White—dramatized this theme. Moreover, there was no final protection against doubts, conflicts, or deep questions about life and work, as Barnard's warning made clear.

Leaders sometimes found that some of their responsibilities conflicted sharply with others. Sometimes, under pressure, they compromised their values to make progress or avoid worse outcomes. Moreover, the stable, less competitive world of many industries did not eliminate uncertainty, anxiety, and competitive pressure. When firms were introducing new products or venturing over-seas, their executives faced risky, complex challenges, rife with uncertainty, and they lost many nights of sleep.

But these leaders often worked in a world that was less risky, more stable, and less competitive than its counter-part today. They worked within an established, familiar superstructure of roles, responsibilities, and purpose. It framed and justified their efforts, and provided guidance when they faced serious pressures and demanding chal-lenges. But today the pressures and challenges are almost continuous. One executive, whose career spanned the last fifty years, commented that work used to consist of peaks and valleys, but now it was all peaks. This is why man-agers and leaders today can experience the question of personal purpose in acute, sometimes painful ways.

The Good Struggle

The personal questions of leadership confront men and women at many levels of organizations, not just at the top. In fact, the final enduring question is almost every-one's question because it is fundamentally a version of the age-old challenge of discerning what counts as a good life. There is no final answer to this question, but there is an emerging perspective that reflects contemporary life as well as traditional wisdom. It offers a measure of insight, guidance, and solace for responsible leaders today.

Surprisingly, the myth of Sisyphus is a valuable starting point for seeking guidance. This story, focused on a bizarre punishment, can seem far removed from life in organizations today. And even if leaders feel, in their low moments, that their work is somehow Sisyphean, that isn't the case in any straightforward way. Their jobs are neither tedious nor monotonous. They work with others, not in bleak solitude, so they have companionship and support. And, despite its pressures, a world with markets everywhere is a world of vast opportunities for initiative, creativity, and reward. With the right skills, hard work, and some luck, leaders can meet their goals and earn the rewards they deserve. In other words, they can keep their rock at the top of the hill.

But the story of Sisyphus has many levels. For centuries, it has captivated thinkers and artists, and they have interpreted it in many different ways. So what does it suggest about a contemporary answer to the last enduring question? The answer involves three basic aspects of the story. Taken together, they suggest a provocative conclusion: that men and women seek positions of leadership and take their responsibilities seriously *because* of the struggles involved, not despite them.

This is perhaps the fundamental reason for thinking about responsible leadership as a good struggle. In other words, responsible leadership is a challenge that—despite its inevitable risks, frustrations, and failures—demands and merits the best efforts of talented men and women, tests their competence and their characters fully, gives purpose and intensity to their lives, and helps them lead the kind of lives they really value. Leaders usually will not make good on all their commitments and aspirations, and their careers may evolve in ways that surprise, disappoint, or seriously dismay them—because the new invisible hand offers few guarantees and because markets are indifferent to the fates of individuals—but the good struggle nevertheless seems worth the risk and cost.

Sheer Hard Work

Recombination can be described in ways that make it sound exciting and fun, and this is often true of the early phases of entrepreneurial innovation, which involve conceiving a project, imagining its possibilities, and sketching a creative combination of people and resources that could bring success. But the reality of successful innovation and creativity was captured in a famous statement made by one of the most creative, practical minds of the last century, the prolific inventor Thomas A. Edison. He said, "Remember, nothing that's good works by itself, just to please you. You have to make the damn thing work."[6]

The image of Sisyphus, straining every muscle to budge a large rock and moving it only inch by inch, is a vivid reminder of the crucial importance of sheer will, the everyday determination and courage of putting one heavy foot in front of the other, and of the almost endless hard work required for accomplishing almost anything of value. In other words, every endeavor that really matters has Sisyphean elements. These are activities that have to be performed, again and again, and that have to meet high, sometimes exacting, and ever-rising standards. These activities occur in the design of a product, crucial aspects of delivering a service, or steady improvements in a manufacturing or service operation.

A market-driven world makes these tasks even harder. Creative recombination in a world of intense performance pressure is hardly a matter of snapping Lego blocks together in colorful, fun structures. In fact, it is probably the most demanding form of management work because it involves providing direction and motivation to other people, many of whom are members of other organizations, each with its own bosses, agendas, uncertainties, and demanding competitive pressures.

Like Sisyphus, the leaders who invest so much of their time, energy, and spirit in these efforts will often watch their rock roll back down the hill, despite their best efforts. Failures, large and small, come with the territory. With luck, these will be "type B" failures. These teach valuable lessons; the parties involved learn them, their commitments and basic direction evolve, and they find other ways to move forward. IBM did this after its near bankruptcy, as do many business founders who fail and live to fight another day. "Type A" failures are different. They are devastating—like the collapse of Bear Stearns and Lehman Brothers—and leave leaders and many others searching through the ruins for anything worth salvaging.

A market-driven world treats everything like an experiment. This is true, of course, for new technologies and new ventures, but even a billion-dollar firm that endures for decades may turn out to be a mere experiment with a particular technology or strategy or type of leadership. All that may survive its failure are lessons for the next group of capitalist innovators. After a failure, it takes courage, determination, and sheer will to go back to work, aim high, work confidently, and bring out the best in others, rather than to retreat and hunker down. The next round of hard work is even harder because the men and women who commit themselves to it now understand, through painful, personal experience, that it can also fail and that the rock may roll back down again, despite their best efforts.

Exercising Vital Capabilities

The standard view is that Sisyphus felt doomed and thought his life was futile, but this is also worth rethinking. The French philosopher Albert Camus, writing in the middle of the last century, suggested that we shouldn't rush to judgment about what Sisyphus thought and felt. Camus concludes a famous essay, "The Myth of Sisyphus," with these words: "The struggle itself toward the heights is enough to fill a man's heart. One must imagine Sisyphus happy."[7]

This is a provocative, perhaps profound perspective. It suggests that, for leaders and others, struggling with really hard challenges isn't a burden. It is, instead, a vital part of their humanity. For them, "fighting the good fight" is a demanding and gratifying way of life. For example, Gary Rogers and a friend acquired a small ice cream company in Oakland, California, in 1977 and built it into a major national company that sells Dreyer's and Edy's ice cream. Looking back over his career, Rogers said simply, "The joy of life is in the struggle." He went on to compare leadership to a crew training in September for a single boat race in April that might last only fifteen minutes. He said, "You have to really like the months of hard, exhausting workouts. Otherwise you don't row, not for that one race, those few minutes, way down the road. It's a good metaphor for life—the best way to achieve your long-term goals is to make the most of every day."[8]

Long before Camus, Aristotle held a similar view. "The good of man," he wrote, "is the active exercise of the soul's faculties in conformity with excellence or virtue."[9] The language is old-fashioned, but the basic concept is timeless. When leaders persevere in hard, uncertain tasks, they are acting with courage and exercising intellectual, emotional, moral, and physical strength. For Aristotle, exercising these vital faculties was an absolute precondition for living fully and well. And the appeal of leadership, despite its demands and struggles, lies in part in the fact that it calls upon the full talents and energy of capable, strong individuals.

If the purpose of life were ease and comfort, no sensible person would take on the demands of leadership. But if Aristotle is correct and the best life involves the full use of human powers, then the demands of leadership today are a daunting but worthwhile way of life. This is why leaders will feel on some days that they have the best jobs in the world and on others like they are at the end of their ropes. This isn't confusion or ambivalence. It is simply acknowledgement that struggle and fulfillment are the two sides of the same valuable coin.

This seems to be true for all leaders—those who make headlines and work at the top of organizations as well as the unnoticed, quiet leaders all around us. With little hesitation, all these men and women put aside ease and comfort to make the world a better place, even though they expect little attention or reward for their effort. While they value money and plaudits, their motives are broader and deeper. They are seeking a way of working and a way of living that enables them to thrive. The search is often unconscious and instinctive, and it may last years or decades. But leaders are often driven forward by a strong sense that the right life for them has serious, challenging responsibilities at its center.

Perhaps the strongest evidence for this perspective is that once many leaders have triumphed or failed, they look for other hard challenges and are frustrated until they find them. Entrepreneurs who sell their companies for huge sums often shun beaches and golf courses and instead start other companies. Others take on the demanding challenges of social entrepreneurship. For these men and women, yesterday's achievements are trophies: valuable, worth admiring occasionally, but bygone and lifeless. Past success pleases them, but new challenges— the next good struggles—captivate them.

Struggle intimidates and invites. It makes the lives of leaders more intense, the failures somewhat less painful, and the successes more gratifying. One executive, who turned around a French manufacturing company despite a long list of challenges, including threats of physical violence, later said, "I wouldn't have missed the job for a million dollars, but I wouldn't do it again for twenty million."[10] In short, demanding challenges give value and purpose to the work and lives of leaders. In the words of the American philosopher and psychologist William James, "Need and struggle are what excite and inspire us."[11]

Reaching for the Heights

Even if a good life and good work depend, to a significant degree, on facing hard challenges and serious demands, it is important to keep struggle in perspective. There is no point banging one's head against a wall, and sometimes the right decision is to step back, rethink a commitment, and move on. And there is little point in seeking out struggles—life brings enough disappointments, hardships, and tragedies to most people. Moreover, some people struggle because they have the wrong skills for a task or because the task is impossible. And some people struggle to achieve frivolous, obnoxious, or evil objectives.

The purpose of a struggle matters crucially. This is why all of the emerging answers to the enduring questions involve close, deep linkages between leaders' struggles and their commitments. The value of the struggle ultimately depends on its purpose. For Sisyphus, as Camus saw him, the aim was reaching "the heights." This gave meaning to his hard and futile labor.

For leaders in a market-driven world, reaching for "the heights" has two very different meanings. One was implicit in the first four enduring questions and the emerging answers to them. "The heights," in this first sense, refer to the actual achievements of leaders and their organizations. This happens when leaders grasp the fundamentals, sharply define their accountability and set the bar high, move their organizations in an evolving, successful direction, and keep their organizations focused on core values. The familiar examples today are the great entrepreneurial success stories, but these often-told tales distract us from the countless examples of small-scale entrepreneurship, creativity, and innovation throughout the economy as well as in the public and social sectors.

The harder these leaders struggle, the better the evidence that they really are truly making a difference in the world. When Machiavelli wrote that there is nothing more dangerous than changing "the order of things," he implicitly suggested that leaders who aren't facing demanding challenges might not be doing much of anything, and some entrepreneurs share this sense. In other words, they feel that real change—the kind that creates the legacy they want—looks hard and is hard, and resistance confirms this. Leaders typically set high standards for themselves. When things come easy, they suspect they aren't really leading.

But "the heights" also has a personal meaning that is crucial to answering the last enduring question. When entrepreneurs initially describe their aims, they often talk about the organizations they want to create, technology that excites them, or a difference they want to make in an industry or community. Also, they usually make clear that they are not monks and want to make money. But when they reflect further, it becomes clear that *how* they achieve these aims is just as important as the aims themselves. Commitment and struggle play a prominent role in these deeper reflections. Put differently, they would not want to wave a magic wand and have their ideal business spring into existence, earning profits, building market share, and operating like a fine Swiss watch.

Entrepreneurs often say that their best years were the really hard years of building their businesses. This was when they were reaching for their own personal heights and becoming the kind of person they aspired to be. They were simultaneously creating organizations and creating themselves. One entrepreneur, for example, said that what he valued most was "cutting his own path in life." Another said that building his business made him feel like a decathlon athlete because he was developing and using a wide range of skills—something he missed in graduate school, when he spent several years on highly specialized life science research. Another said he thought that he and many other entrepreneurs liked fighting and beating the "status quo." Another said he wanted to be the center forward who got the ball on the soccer field when the game was on the line.[12]

In short, taking on hard challenges helps men and women understand who they really are, the values and dreams they are willing to make sacrifices for, their true skills and talents, the work they must do, and the trade-offs they will and won't make. Despite his many successes, Steve Jobs once reflected, "There are many moments that are filled with despair and agony, when you have to fire people and cancel things and deal with very difficult situations. That's when you find out who you are and what your values are."[13]

Leaders who work in large organizations often feel the same way. One former executive said that he thought a good deal of merger and acquisition activity took place simply because CEOs were no longer actually running an operation themselves, as they did earlier in their careers. Instead, they were managing other people who had the hands-on challenge and satisfaction of managing businesses, divisions, and large operations. As a result, he thought, some CEOs began buying and selling parts of businesses to gain a feeling they were actually doing something.

Whether leaders are entrepreneurs or not, the challenges of leadership enable them to reach for their own personal heights. How they meet these challenges says something important—to the world and to themselves—about the kind of people they are. They take pride in being confident, optimistic, determined people who can get things done, particularly when others think a task is very hard. Gary Rogers, the founder of Dreyer's Grand Ice Cream, said his lifelong personal creed was "There is no such thing as 'can't,' only 'won't.'"[14]

This spirit is why many entrepreneurs continue trying to start businesses, even after other ventures have failed, and why leaders in organizations of all kinds persevere, set ambitious goals, and even dream, despite serious setbacks. They see themselves, consciously or unconsciously, as the kind of person who forges ahead, especially in the face of adversity. And they don't want to simply *see* themselves this way—they want to *be* this kind of person.

Notice that "the heights" defined in personal terms has little to do with getting rich. Like almost everyone else, entrepreneurs prefer success and enjoy its rewards. But their motives for taking on really hard and uncertain struggles run much deeper. They are complexly intertwined with how they want to live, how they see themselves, and what they want to become.

As Aristotle suggested, the allure of struggle may be part of human nature. It may even be genetic: presumably, the early humans and prehumans who were not disposed to struggle died off more quickly, on barren savannahs and in dangerous jungles, and didn't pass along their DNA. But Aristotle's insight was much broader than evolutionary theory. For him, struggle and the courage to struggle were the foundation of a life well lived, regardless of whether a person was a leader.

Hard challenges help leaders understand who they are and become what they hope to be. Serious commitments and the struggles they bring help men and women develop patience, courage, determination, and confidence. And serious challenges can lead to lives of greater clarity, awareness, and intensity. Henry David Thoreau found this when he lived in an isolated cabin through two New England winters. He later wrote, "I went to the woods because I wished to live deliberately, to front only the essential facts of life, and see if I could not learn what it had to teach, and not, when I came to die, discover that I had not lived. I did not wish to live what was not life, living is so dear."[15]

The Burden of Freedom

The central theme of this book can be summarized in two short statements: responsible leadership is commitment, and commitment is struggle. The first statement may seem true but obvious, but commitment is much more than a bit of vague, inspirational rhetoric. It is a complex, multifaceted idea with strong, practical implications for leaders today, and the emerging answers to the enduring questions show this.

The second statement may seem wrong to those who think about leadership in terms of confidence, optimism, hope, and inspiration. But that view is, at best, an incomplete picture of the larger challenges and everyday work of responsible leadership. Leaders do, of course, have moments of elation and stretches of smooth sailing, but in the exciting, turbulent, and dangerous world of the new invisible hand, these moments can be infrequent and fleeting, and they are typically hard won—through very demanding effort and real struggle.

A market-driven economy frees us to choose and commit in ways that the old, stable hierarchies didn't. The organization man could hope to get on a corporate escalator and then—with hard work, the right mentors, astute politics, and luck—rise steadily higher. But today's freedom is also a burden. A fluid world of abundant opportunity can leave leaders feeling they are on their own, dealing with remorseless competition and almost incessant change—a hefty price for the abundant opportunities for creativity, invention, entrepreneurship, and self-determination.

In this world, the enduring questions of responsible leadership are especially valuable. They put a bright light on the basic challenges responsible leaders face: grasping the fundamentals, defining their accountability, getting critical decisions right, making a few crucial values real and effective in an organization, and finding purpose, guidance, and solace for what is often a long, hard journey. Each of the enduring questions points to a demanding struggle. None of the questions is ever answered, finally and permanently, by an individual leader or a society. But thinking hard about these questions can help leaders raise the odds of working successfully and responsibly in the exciting, uncertain, recombinant, market-driven world all around us.

RESEARCH BACKGROUND

The basic aim of this project was to learn about responsible leadership in a turbulent, market-driven world by studying entrepreneurs. To accomplish this, I viewed their experiences and reflections from three different perspectives.

First, I read and analyzed seventy-five case studies on entrepreneurs to learn about the full range of issues involving leadership and responsibility that they faced. These cases typically described individuals who had created and led new organizations during the last decade or so. I tried to include entrepreneurs from a wide range of companies, home countries, and industries. In the process of doing this, I also reflected on my personal experience with entrepreneurs. This consisted of several case studies I had written about new ventures and small companies, as well as serving for several years on the boards of two start-up companies.

Second, I read and analyzed the experiences of an additional fifty entrepreneurs whose efforts were described in serious books. Some of the entrepreneurs worked in recent decades, others a century or more ago. Some of their firms, such as General Motors, U.S. Steel, and

FedEx, are best known as giant enterprises, but all of them were initially small, fragile, entrepreneurial ventures, and their founders and early leaders typically faced highly uncertain, complex, and dangerous environments.

Among the historical studies I consulted, these were the most valuable:

Dan Briody, *The Halliburton Agenda: The Politics of Oil and Money* (Hoboken, NJ: Wiley, 2004)

A'Lelia Bundles, *On Her Own Ground: The Life and Times of Madam C. J. Walker* (New York: Scribner, 2001)

Lisa Chaney, *Coco Chanel: An Intimate Life* (New York: Viking, 2011)

Peter Chapman, *Bananas: How the United Fruit Company Shaped the World* (Edinburgh, UK: Canongate, 2009).

Charles W. Cheape, *Family Firm to Modern Multinational: Norton Company, a New England Enterprise* (Cambridge, MA: Harvard University Press, 1985)

Ron Chernow, *Titan: The Life of John D. Rockefeller, Sr.* (New York: Random House, 1998)

Harald van B. Cleveland and Thomas F. Huertas, *Citibank, 1812–1970* (Cambridge, MA: Harvard University Press, 1985)

Niel Dahlstrom and Jeremy Dahlstrom, *The John Deere Story: A Biography of Plowmakers John and*

Charles Deere (DeKalb: Northern Illinois University Press, 2005)

Henry Ford, *My Life and Work* (Garden City, NY: Doubleday, Page, 1922)

Roger Frock, *Changing How the World Does Business: FedEx's Incredible Journey to Success* (San Francisco: Berrett-Koehler, 2006)

Masaaki Sato, *The Toyota Leaders: An Executive Guide*, trans. Justin Bonsey (New York: Vertical, 2008)

Alfred P. Sloan, Jr., *My Years with General Motors*, ed. John McDonald, with Catharine Stevens (Garden City, NY: Doubleday, 1964)

T. J. Stiles, *The First Tycoon: The Epic Life of Cornelius Vanderbilt* (New York: Alfred A. Knopf, 2009)

Joseph Wall, *Andrew Carnegie* (New York: Oxford University Press, 1970)

The third phase of my research was unusual and re- markably valuable. I had initially planned to interview a significant number of entrepreneurs, as a complement to the cases and books I was studying. And this is what I eventually did, but I focused the interviews in a particu- lar way.

For several decades, Harvard Business School has had a major commitment to studying and teaching about en- trepreneurship, and more than thirty faculty members now teach dozens of courses on the subject. I decided that another way to gain insight on the questions I was studying would be interviewing my colleagues in the Entrepreneurship Unit and a good number of the entrepreneurs-in-residence they had carefully recruited. These interviews provided an extraordinarily deep and broad perspective on entrepreneurship generally and on the issues of struggle, commitment, and managerial courage.

The faculty members and entrepreneurs had served— in many cases, for decades—as founders of one or more companies, directors of many start-ups and small firms, investors in this type of firm, or managers of venture capital and other investment companies. In addition, my colleagues had been studying, writing case studies, giving lectures, and writing both practical and scholarly articles on entrepreneurship for most of their careers. Their cumulative experience reflected extended work with hundreds, perhaps thousands, of entrepreneurs and small new companies, in a wide range of industries and countries, over many decades.

In my interviews with the entrepreneurs-in-residence, the initial focus was the company the entrepreneur had started, but we soon moved to the basic themes of this book—commitment, struggle, and moments of courage. This meant a good deal of the interview time was spent on hard stretches and seemingly lost situations, rather than on periods of triumph, camaraderie, and creativity.

The names of the colleagues and entrepreneurs I interviewed are in the acknowledgments that follow this section, with the exception of some entrepreneurs who asked me to keep their interviews confidential, typically because they involved difficult personnel decisions and company failures.

In short, this third perspective on entrepreneurship enabled me to take advantage of an extraordinary wealth of experience, knowledge, insight, and reflection on the work and challenges facing men and women who start and run new companies. I was able to move far beyond what I was learning from case studies and books on entrepreneurs, as well as from conventional interview strategies, which usually have a sharp focus on the experiences of a single individual and a particular organization.

This was particularly valuable, given the type of book I aimed to write. I am hardly an expert on entrepreneurship, and a few years of part-time study wouldn't make me one. My objective was to write an essay, rather than to provide definitive research findings. This book aims to suggest new perspectives, stimulate and provoke, and cautiously offer practical guidance. Extended dialogue with colleagues and entrepreneurs with broad experience added immeasurably to the effort.

NOTES

CHAPTER ONE

1. Dag Hammarskjöld, *Markings* (New York: Alfred A. Knopf, 1964). For a brief discussion of Hammarskjöld's views of responsibility, see Gustaf Aalen, *Dag Hammarskjöld's White Book* (Philadelphia: Fortress Press, 1969), 104–112.

2. For a provocative, wide-ranging critique of the societal influence of markets and market-based thinking, see Michael J. Sandel, *What Money Can't Buy* (New York: Farrar, Straus and Giroux, 2011).

3. The original German version is "Erst kommt das Fressen, dann kommt die Moral." This is variously translated as "Grub first, then ethics," "First comes a full stomach, then comes ethics," "Chow comes first; morality second," and "First comes feeding, then morality." See Bertolt Brecht, *The Threepenny Opera*, act 2, scene 6.

4. Roger Frock, *Changing How the World Does Business* (San Francisco: Berrett-Koehler, 2006), ix.

5. Schumpeter's views on what kind of firm drives recombination and "creative destruction" are difficult to pin down because, over the course of several decades and several books, he argued that small, entrepreneurial firms played this role and that huge firms, which could finance costly R&D and take a long-term perspective, were the true engines of innovation. See Richard Langlois, *The Dynamics of Industrial Capitalism* (London: Routledge, 2007), 17–18.

6. While entrepreneurship has received a good deal of attention in the press and academia in recent decades, the most recent era of entrepreneurial firms backed by venture capital began in the middle of the twentieth century, with the creation of the first venture capital firms. But they needed decades to become a significant financial force, which reflects, in part, how deeply entrenched and powerful the

established ways of doing business had become. See Spencer Ante, *Creative Capital: George Doriot and the Birth of Venture Capital* (Boston: Harvard Business School Press, 2008).

CHAPTER TWO

1. Arthur C. Clarke, *Profiles of the Future; an Inquiry into the Limits of the Possible* (New York: Harper & Row, 1973).

2. Tarun Khanna, *Billions of Entrepreneurs: How China and India Are Reshaping Their Futures and Yours* (Boston: Harvard Business School Press, 2008).

3. See "17 Who Fell Off the List," *Fortune*, December 10, 2007, 133. For CEO turnover during earlier decades, see Mark Hudson, Robert Parrino, and Laura Starks, "Internal Monitoring Mechanisms and CEO Turnover: A Long-Term Perspective," *Journal of Finance* 56 (2001): 2265–2297. For the last two decades, see Steven Kaplan and Bernadette Minton, "How Has CEO Turnover Changed?" working paper NBER 12465, National Bureau of Economic Research, Cambridge, MA, August 2008.

4. Commission of the European Communities, *Green Paper: Entrepreneurship in Europe* 9 (2003), at http://eur-lex.europa.eu/ LexUriServ/site/en/com/2003/com2003_0027en01.pdf. While accurate, statements like this are only partial glimpses of the complex changes continuously underway in developed economies and the difficulties of summarizing them in any single index. See Dane Stangler and Sam Arbesman, "What Does Fortune 500 Turnover Mean?" (Kansas City, MO: Ewing Marion Kauffman Foundation, 2012).

5. Justin Lahart, "U.S. Firms Build Up Record Cash Piles," *The Wall Street Journal*, June 10, 2010.

6. Nicholas Varchaver, "What Warren Thinks," *Fortune*, April 14, 2008.

7. An insightful overview and critique of techniques for strategic thinking is Walter Kiechel, *The Lords of Strategy* (Boston: Harvard Business School Press, 2010).

8. Richard J. Connors, *Warren Buffett on Business: Principles from the Sage of Omaha* (Hoboken, NJ: John Wiley & Sons, 2010), 143.

9. William Shakespeare, *Julius Caesar*, act 4, scene 3, lines 218–224.

10. Alfred D. Chandler, *The Visible Hand: The Managerial Revolution in American Business* (Cambridge, MA: Belknap Press of Harvard University Press, 1993). The giant hierarchies developed and controlled critical technology. In fact, organizational hierarchies were actually a critical technology, albeit a "soft" one. The capacity to measure, monitor, and control the performance of managers, as well as the machinery and factories for which they were accountable, was as important to economic growth as the "hard" technologies of engines, modern chemistry, and electronics. This was part of a broader trend in society, one that Max Weber, the renowned sociologist, called "bureaucratic rationality"—the imposing of control systems and logical rules on various spheres of human activity. The displacement of traditional relationships, based on history, community, and kinship, by rational, purposeful, efficient systems was a major theme in Weber's work. See, for example, Max Weber, *General Economic History* (Mineola, NY: Dover Publications, 2003).

11. See, for example, Max Weber and Talcott Parsons, *The Theory of Social and Economic Organization* (New York: Free Press, 1997), 340.

12. The ambivalence about these extraordinarily powerful and productive economic units was described at length in a classic book, published at the moment when their power had perhaps peaked. See John Kenneth Galbraith, *The New Industrial State* (Boston: Houghton Mifflin, 1967). Galbraith was a highly regarded Harvard economist and public intellectual, and he argued that large corporations, for well and ill, were the prototype of the future.

13. A conceptual overview of this perspective and the ongoing debate about markets and organizations today is Richard N. Langlois, "The Dynamics of Industrial Capitalism," in J. Stanley Metcalfe, *Evolutionary Economics and Creative Destruction* (London: Routledge, 1998).

14. There are extensive literatures on modularity in a broad and growing range of fields, including computer science, mathematics, cognitive neuroscience, ecology, biology, and architecture. Basic accounts of modularity focus on the evolution or design of modules and, in addition, the creation of interfaces and standards that enable modules to be linked to each other. A theoretical treatment of

modularity, from the perspective of economics and industrial design, is Carliss Baldwin and Kim Clark, *Design Rules* (Cambridge, MA: MIT Press, 2000).

15. Jena McGregor, "GE's Immelt: An Even Hotter Throne," *BusinessWeek*, July 16, 2008, 36.

16. The comment was made at an off-the-record seminar at Harvard Business School in March 2006. Looking even more broadly, a common view is that innovation is primarily the creation of wholly new ideas or the invention of unprecedented products or services and that recombination is a much easier and basically inferior form of innovation. But the recent trend in scholarship on innovation strongly suggests otherwise. For one thing, recombination of complex technologies, capabilities, or services requires skill and talent. For another, most innovation may actually consist of creative recombination. In fact, there are deeper philosophical reasons to conclude that *all* innovation is the inevitable result of "conceptual blending," which can naturally be construed as a form of recombination. See Mark Turner and Gilles Fauconnier, "Conceptual Integration and Formal Expression," *Metaphor and Symbolic Activity* 10, no. 3 (1995): 183–204.

17. An early, extended documentation of this phenomenon was Arlie Hochschild, *The Time Bind* (New York: Holt Paperbacks, 2001).

18. There is considerable controversy over whether individuals today have more careers than their predecessors, and the answer turns, in part, on how "career" and "job" are defined. For an overview, see Carl Bialik, "Seven Careers in a Lifetime? Think Twice, Researchers Say," *The Wall Street Journal*, September 4, 2010. For basic statistical data, see the National Longitudinal Survey, Bureau of Labor Statistics, http://www.bls.gov/nls/home.htm.

19. The first use of this term appears to be Barbara Kantrowitz, "In Search of the Sacred," *Newsweek*, November, 1994, 52–62.

20. One of the leading Al Qaeda theorists, Abu Musab al-Suri, has written, "*Jihadis* should avoid creating hierarchical structures, which are vulnerable to attack by local or American security forces, and move instead to a decentralized system of individuals or small local cells linked only by ideology." *The Economist*, November 1, 2007.

21. Some analysts see these forces from an environmental perspective. See, for example, Paul Gilding, *The Great Disruption* (New York: Bloomsbury Press, 2011). Others focus on information technology, such as John Hagel and John Seely Brown, *The Power of Pull* (New York: Basic Books, 2010). Others on socioeconomic transitions: Tyler Cowen, *The Great Stagflation* (New York: Dutton Adult, 2011). And some on sweeping cultural and intellectual changes: Daniel T. Rogers, *Age of Fracture* (Cambridge, MA: Belknap Press of Harvard University Press, 2011). Rogers's overview of contemporary life is this: "On both the intellectual right and the intellectual left, earlier notions of history and society that stressed solidity, collective institutions, and social circumstances gave way to a more individualized human nature that emphasized choice, agency, performance, and desire . . . Structures of power came to seem less important than market choice and fluid selves."

22. Japan is an important test case for the scope and power of these forces. For decades, it was a brilliant economic success, but market forces were controlled and guided by government agencies, industrial policy, and longstanding networks of relationships among banks, industrial companies, and their suppliers. Now there are many signs that these relationships are eroding and that their replacements are market relationships. See Stephen Vogel, *Japan Remodeled: How Government and Industry Are Reforming Japanese Capitalism* (Ithaca, NY: Cornell University Press, 2006).

23. A recent survey found that only 15 percent of companies in North America and Japan believe they have enough qualified personnel to fill key positions; the European number was 30 percent. See Claudio Fernandez-Araoz, Boris Groysberg, and Nitin Nohria, "How to Hang On to Your High Potentials," *Harvard Business Review*, October 2011, 76.

24. For example, postings on social media sites can be used to signal labor market availability without alerting one's employers. As one individual put it, "You are always looking for the next job. No matter how good the current one is. You just don't know what you are going to get offered. You just have to be careful how you do it." See Mikolaj Jan Piskorski, Harvard Business School, "Networks as Covers: Evidence from an On-line Social Network," unpublished working paper. And, as their experiences become more varied, they

often become even more attractive to future employers. See Ali McConnon and Jessica Silver-Greenberg, "Meet the New Recruits: They Want to Eat Your Lunch," *Business Week*, May 15, 2008. This article quotes a senior executive at a major investment firm who says, "If you are specialized too early, there is a risk you will be less innovative because you have fewer building blocks to combine in new ways."

25. The value of this information is indicated by company efforts to block its dissemination. See, for example, Josh Gerstein, "Under the Radar," *Politico*, February 9, 2011.

26. See Andrew Morse, "IDEC-Biogen Feels Like Big Pharma," *The Daily Deal*, June 25, 2003.

27. Dan Briody, *The Halliburton Agenda* (New York: Wiley, 2005), 71.

28. The sophistication of corporate political strategies is both remarkable and unnerving. For example, one study found that firms with extensive outsourcing activities modified their accounting accruals to limit scrutiny in election years. See Karthik Ramana and Sugata Roychowdhury, "Elections and Discretionary Accruals: Evidence from 2004," *Journal of Accounting Research* 48, no. 2 (May 2010): 445–475. The power of these strategies is also unnervingly impressive. In 2008, for example, the American Petroleum Institute started a public relations campaign, which may have cost nearly $100 million, to persuade Americans that increased crude oil prices and not record oil company profits were responsible for recent increases in energy costs. The campaign was intended to counter the view, promulgated by industry critics, that the major oil companies did not deserve the tax allowances it had and that, as one member of Congress put it, "big oil" was a "one-word epithet." See Jeffrey Binbaum, "Oil Lobby Reaches Out to Citizens Peeved at the Pump," *BusinessWeek*, May 9, 2008.

29. For an extended explanation, see Alison Gropnik, Andrew Meltzoff, and Patricia Kuhl, *In the Crib: What Early Learning Tells Us about the Mind* (New York: HarperCollins, 2001), 85ff.

30. In doing so, companies and other organizations are sometimes exercising power in sophisticated, subtle, but powerful ways. The sociologist Steven Lukes has made what is now a classic distinction among three dimensions of power. The first two—influencing particular decisions and influencing decision-making institutions—are familiar and are used by companies and other organizations

competing in the market for government influence. The third level involves shaping norms and values that may not be considered consciously but serve as permanent filters on what people observe and how they make value judgments. See Steven Lukes, *Power: A Radical View* (New York: Palgrave Macmillan, 2004).

31. "An Evening with Legendary Venture Capitalist Arthur Rock in Conversation with John Markoff," Computer History Museum, May 10, 2012, 16, http://archive.computerhistory.org/resources/access/text/2012/05/102658253-05-01-acc.pdf.

32. Friedrich Nietzsche, *Human, All Too Human: A Book for Free Spirits*, trans. Alexander Harvey (Chicago: Charles H. Kerr, 1908), 71–72.

33. Jeff Bussgang, general partner, Flybridge Capital Associates, interview by author, April 1, 2011.

34. James Sharpe, former CEO, Extrusion Technologies, interview by author, April 19, 2011.

35. Professor William Sahlman, Harvard Business School, interview by author, May 11, 2001.

36. Howard Stevenson, interview by author, May 3, 2011.

37. Oliver Wendell Holmes and Richard A. Posner, *The Essential Holmes: Selections from the Letters, Speeches, Judicial Opinions, and Other Writings of Oliver Wendell Holmes, Jr.* (Chicago: University of Chicago, 1996), 82.

CHAPTER THREE

1. Arthur O. Lovejoy, *The Great Chain of Being: A Study of the History of an Idea* (Cambridge, MA: Harvard University Press, 1966).

2. The early, authoritative statement of this issue was E. Merrick Dodd, Jr., "For Whom Are Corporate Managers Trustees?" *Harvard Law Review* 45, no. 7 (May 1932). The best-known popular statement of the shareholder view is Milton Friedman, "The Social Responsibility of Business Is to Increase Its Profits," *The New York Times Magazine*, September 13, 1970. A powerful elaboration of these basic ideas, both conceptually and practically, appeared six years later: Michael C. Jensen and William H. Meckling, "Theory of the Firm: Managerial Behavior, Agency Costs and Ownership Structure," *Journal of Financial Economics* 3, no. 4 (October 1976): 305–360. There

are many versions of the stakeholder view. The comprehensive modern statement is R. Edward Freeman, *Strategic Management: A Stakeholder Approach* (Cambridge: Cambridge University Press, 2010). Another version of the stakeholder view, with an emphasis on knowledge-based economies, is Charles Handy, "What's a Business For?" *Harvard Business Review*, November–December 2002. The debate has been further complicated by scholars who advocate the primacy of other stakeholders, such as customers. See, for example, Roger Martin, "The Age of Customer Capitalism," *Harvard Business Review*, January–February 2010. A historical treatment of these issues, which argues that each side of the debate waxes and wanes as a result of varying social, economic, and political developments, is William T. Allen, "Our Schizophrenic Conception of the Business Corporation," *Cardozo Law Review* 14 (1992): 261.

3. Private communication at Harvard Business School symposium on governance, November 2004.

4. Private communication to author, March 2006.

5. See, for example, Lucian A. Bebchuk and Yaniv Grinstein, "The Growth of Executive Pay," *Oxford Review of Economic Policy* 21, no. 2 (2005): 283–303. The authors analyze very large samples of US firms between 1993 and 2003 and find that the pay of the top five executives rose much more rapidly than changes in firm size or industry classification would explain. Their conclusion is that a hard-to-specify mix of market forces and managerial power explains this development. The bibliography and footnotes in the article provide a broad overview of the academic debate on executive compensation and its driving forces.

6. Strong, often harsh critiques of board governance are easy to find, and many originate with "insiders" who have served on many corporate boards. See, for example, William Bowen, *The Board Book* (New York: W. W. Norton, 2008), 179. Bowen, the former president of Princeton University and a former board member of American Express, Merck, and several other public and private organizations, recently commented that "boards need to be less supine"—a goal for improvement that suggests prevailing practice is mediocre, almost a decade after the Sarbanes-Oxley reforms.

7. *The Economist*, hardly a foe of capitalism or corporations, reported: "The Securities and Exchange Commission recently proposed

a tiny rule change to make it slightly easier for shareholders to nominate candidates for election to boards of directors. Lobbyists representing America's top bosses easily and unceremoniously killed the proposal. Look no further to see where the real power still resides in corporate America." See "Bossing the Bosses," *The Economist*, April 7, 2005. And, even when activist shareholders succeed in bringing about a vote, the outcome—support for positions supported by the CEO—is usually overwhelming and predetermined, like elections in the old East Germany. Only acute crises lead to changes in CEOs and board membership, and, at this point, companies have often been seriously or irreparably damaged. A study of shareholder votes by Michael Jensen, a highly respected scholar and a long-time advocate of free-market capitalism, led him to conclude, "[I]n American companies, the CEO effectively has no boss. He or she is the boss unless or until there is an outside crisis that threatens the reputations of people on the board. Then the power shifts, the board members become the bosses, and you see people getting fired. But by that time there is a whole lot of value destroyed that may not be recoverable." Michael Jensen, *Journal of Applied Corporate Finance* 20, no. 1 (2008): 29.

8. A detailed account of the philosophy, leadership, and operations of this company is found in Sandra Sucher, Daniela Beyersdorfer, and Ane Damgaard Jensen, "Generation Investment Management," Case 9-609-057 (Boston: Harvard Business School, 2012).

9. See V. Kasturi Rangan, "The Aravind Eye Hospital in Madurai, India: In Service for Sight," Case 9-593-098 (Boston: Harvard Business School, 1993), 1.

10. See Heerad Sabeti, "The For-Benefit Enterprise," *Harvard Business Review*, November 2011. See also "Firms with Benefits," *The Economist*, January 7, 2012.

11. David Bornstein, "The Rise of the Social Entrepreneur," *The New York Times*, November 13, 2012, 20.

12. This approach to corporate responsibility has been called "shared value creation." A clear, forceful elaboration of this approach to corporate social responsibility is Michael E. Porter and Mark R. Kramer, "Strategy and Society: The Link between Competitive Advantage and Corporate Social Responsibility," *Harvard Business Review*, December 2006.

13. Walter Isaacson, *Steve Jobs* (New York: Simon & Schuster, 2011), 535.

14. For an extended, contemporary treatment of this perspective on moral philosophy—focused on the ethics of individuals, not corporations—see Richard Kraut, *What Is Good and Why: The Ethics of Well-Being* (Cambridge, MA: Harvard University Press, 2009).

15. David Lilienthal, *Management: A Humanist Art* (New York: Columbia University Press, 1967), 18.

CHAPTER FOUR

1. Drucker's full statement was, "If objectives are only good intentions, they are worthless. They must degenerate into work." Peter F. Drucker, *Management: Tasks, Responsibilities, Practices*, revised ed. (New York: HarperCollins, 2008), 127.

2. Napoleon Bonaparte, *Napoleon's Letters to Josephine, 1796–1812*, trans. Henry F. Hall (New York: E.P. Dutton, 1901), 207.

3. Ron Chernow, *Titan: The Life of John D. Rockefeller, Sr.* (New York: Vintage, 2004), 102.

4. Andrew S. Grove, *Only the Paranoid Survive: How to Exploit the Crisis Points That Challenge Every Company* (New York: Crown Business, 1999).

5. Morten Hansen, "Three Leadership Skills That Count," HBR Blog Network, October 20, 2011, http://blogs.hbr.org/cs/2011/10/three_leadership_skills_that_c.html.

6. Noam Wasserman, *The Founder's Dilemmas* (Princeton, NJ: Princeton University Press, 2012), 58.

7. Gary Mueller, CEO of Institutional Investor and founder of ISI Emerging Markets, interview by author, March 11, 2011.

8. Michael C. Jensen and William H. Meckling, "The Theory of the Firm: Managerial Behavior, Agency Costs, and Ownership Structure," *Journal of Financial Economics* 3, no. 4 (October 1976): 305–360.

9. A careful, in-depth study of entrepreneurs by Professor Saras Sarasvathy of the University of Virginia concluded that entrepreneurs relied heavily on "effectual reasoning." Instead of starting with a precise set of goals, they use their personal strengths as a foundation and then respond flexibly and creatively to opportunities. See Leigh Buchanan, "How Great Entrepreneurs Think," *Inc.*, February 1, 2011.

10. Carl von Clausewitz, *On War*, trans. J. J. Graham, ed. F. N. Maude (Radford, VA: Wilder Publications, 2008), 61.

11. Professor Amy Edmondson of Harvard Business School has written extensively about this perspective and on broader aspects of organizational learning. In 2008 she wrote: "[E]ven flawless execution cannot guarantee enduring success in the knowledge economy. The influx of new knowledge in most fields makes it easy to fall behind. Consider General Motors—the largest, most profitable company in the world in the early 1970s. Confident of the wisdom of its approach, GM remained wedded to a well-developed competency in centralized control and high-volume execution. Despite this, the firm steadily lost ground in subsequent decades and posted a record $38.7 billion loss in 2007. Like many dominant companies in the industrial era, General Motors was slow to understand that great execution is difficult to sustain—not because people get tired of working hard, but because the managerial mind-set that enables efficient execution inhibits employees' ability to learn and innovate. A focus on getting things done, and done right, crowds out the experimentation and reflection vital to sustainable success." See Amy Edmondson, "The Competitive Imperative of Learning," *Harvard Business Review*, July 2008.

12. Professor Lynda Applegate, Harvard Business School, interview by author, May 5, 2011.

13. Shikhar Ghosh, founder and former CEO of Open Market, interview by author, May 9, 2011.

14. Robert Higgins, cofounder and general partner, Highland Capital Partners, interview by author, May 18, 2011.

15. Ghosh interview, May 9, 2011.

16. Lao-tzu, trans. by Stephen Mitchell, *Tao Te Ching* (New York: Harper Perennial, 2009), passage 77.

17. See Chernow, *Titan*, 130.

18. Joseph Wall, *Andrew Carnegie* (Pittsburgh: University of Pennsylvania Press, 1989), 342.

19. Professor Howard Stevenson, interview by author, May 3, 2011.

20. Admiral Hyman Rickover gave President Kennedy a plaque with this prayer engraved on it, which Kennedy kept on his desk in the Oval Office. Rickover had given similar plaques to commanders of new submarines under his command. Gerhard Peters and John T.

Woolley, The American Presidency Project, http://www.presidency
.ucsb.edu/ws/?pid=9234.

CHAPTER FIVE

1. Robert Nozick, *Anarchy, State, and Utopia* (New York: Basic Books, 1977), 163.

2. William H. Whyte, *The Organization Man* (Philadelphia: University of Pennsylvania Press, 2002).

3. Linda A. Hill, Jennifer M. Suesse, and Mara Willard, "Franco Bernabe at ENI (A)," Case 9-498-434, video short (Boston: Harvard Business School, 2002).

4. M. Forster, T. Ploughman, and B. McDonald, "Commonality in Codes of Ethics," working paper, University of Notre Dame, 2008.

5. Bill Gates, interview by David Allison, National Museum of American History, 1995, http://americanhistory.si.edu/collections/comphist/gates.htm.

6. Catherine Arnst, "IBM: A Work in Progress," *BusinessWeek*, August 9, 1993.

7. Lynn Paine, Rohit Deshpandé, Joshua D. Margolis, and Kim Eric Batcher, "Up to Code? Does Your Company's Conduct Meet World-Class Standards?" *Harvard Business Review*, December 2005.

8. Confidential communication, fall, 2012.

9. Louis D. Brandeis, "What Publicity Can Do," *Harper's Weekly*, December 20, 1913, 10.

10. Christopher Michel, managing director of Nautilus Ventures, founder of Affinity Labs, interview by author, March 8, 2011.

11. There is a long, rich, complex literature on this topic. A good overview, which draws on the work of one of the pioneers who developed this perspective, is D. Campbell, ed., *The Relational Theory of Contract: Selected Works of Ian Macneil* (London: Sweet & Maxwell, 2001).

12. Elliot Schrage, prepared statement for hearing "The Internet in China: A Tool for Freedom or Suppression?" Committee on International Relations, U.S. House of Representatives, February 15, 2006.

13. Clayton Christensen, an authority on competition and innovation, has concluded that many innovation efforts start out in the wrong direction and are best corrected by market forces, under conditions of limited resources. "How Hard Times Can Drive Innovation," *The Wall Street Journal*, December 15, 2008.

14. Sarika Bansal, "The Power of Failure," *The New York Times*, November 28, 2012, http://opinionator.blogs.nytimes.com/2012/11/28/the-power-of-failure-2/.

15. Janet Kraus, cofounder of Circles, interview by author, May 18, 2011.

16. See Baruch Lev, "How to Win Investors Over," *Harvard Business Review*, November 2011. Michael Jensen, for three decades a widely respected authority on financial markets and management, has said, "[M]anagers think they have to engage in this game; if they don't, the capital markets will ignore them and their values will collapse. But I think the exact opposite is true. If they stopped guiding earnings and started a more substantive, forward-looking, strategic dialogue with investors, they would find themselves with a more sophisticated—and probably a more loyal—shareholder base." "U.S. Corporate Governance: Accomplishments and Failings: A Discussion with Michael Jensen and Robert Monks," in Donald H. Chew and Stuart L. Gillan (eds.), *U.S. Corporate Governance* (New York: Columbia University Press, 2009), p. 68.

17. Personal communication with Ed Zschau, October 7, 2012.

18. Rob Goffee and Gareth Jones, "Leading Clever People," *Harvard Business Review*, March 2007.

19. See Teresa Amabile and Steven Kramer, *The Progress Principle* (Boston: Harvard Business Press, 2011).

20. Warren Buffett, presentation to Salomon Brothers employees, August 26, 1991.

21. Muhammad Ali and Hana Yasmeen Ali, *The Soul of a Butterfly: Reflections on Life's Journey* (New York: Simon & Schuster, 2004), 72.

22. New York Financial Writers Association, prepared remarks of US Attorney Preet Bharara, June 6, 2011, CUNY School of Journalism, New York.

CHAPTER SIX

1. Personal communication with Daniel Callahan, October 11, 2011.

2. Job 14:1–2, as quoted in Robert Alter, *The Wisdom Books: Job, Proverbs, and Ecclesiastes: A Translation with Commentary* (New York: W.W. Norton, 2011), 62.

3. Niccolò Machiavelli, *The Prince* (London: Penguin Books, 1988), 51.

4. Chester A. Barnard, *The Functions of the Executive* (Cambridge, MA: Harvard University Press, 1982), 278.

5. The actual statement, which was made by former GM President Charles "Charlie Engine" Wilson at the US Senate hearings on his nomination to be US secretary of defense in 1953, was a reply to a question asking if, as defense secretary, he could make a decision that harmed General Motors. Wilson said, "I cannot conceive of one, because for years I thought what was good for our country was good for General Motors and vice versa. The difference did not exist. Our company is too big. It goes with the welfare of the country.'" See http://www.freep.com/article/20080914/BUSINESS01/809140308/GM-s-Engine-Charlie-Wilson-learned-live-misquote.

6. M. A. Rosanoff, "Edison in His Laboratory," *Harper's Bazaar*, September 1932, 402.

7. Albert Camus, trans. by Justin O'Brien, *The Myth of Sisyphus and Other Essays* (New York: Vintage, 1991), 123.

8. T. Gary Rogers, cofounder, Dreyer's Grand Ice Cream, interview by author, May 18, 2011.

9. Aristotle, *Nicomachean Ethics*, trans. H. Rackham (Cambridge, MA: Harvard University Press, 2003), 39.

10. Christopher A. Bartlett, "Ideal Standard France: Pat Paterson," video, product number 883512-VID-ENG (Boston: Harvard Business School, 1982).

11. William James, *Is Life Worth Living?* (Philadelphia: S. Burns Weston, 1896), 32.

12. The comments from entrepreneurs are from confidential parts of interviews with them. Noam Wasserman, *The Founder's Dilemmas* (Princeton, NJ: Princeton University Press, 2012), 12–35, provides a valuable quantitative analysis of entrepreneurs' motivations.

13. Steve Jobs, "Apple's One-Dollar-a-Year Man," *Fortune*, January 24, 2000.

14. Rogers interview.

15. Henry David Thoreau, *Walden* (New York: New American Library, 1960), 66.

INDEX

ACKNOWLEDGMENTS

This short book emerged after a long effort—in many ways, a struggle—that spanned five years. I am deeply grateful to many of my colleagues and to others for their suggestions and support all along the way.

Some colleagues helped directly with my effort to understand entrepreneurs and their work. I am particularly grateful to Lynda Applegate, Tom Eisenmann, Shikhar Ghosh, Richard Hamermesh, Bruce Harreld, Bob Higgins, Joe Lassiter, Mike Roberts, and Noam Wasserman. In addition, over the course of this project I had several long, valuable conversations with Howard Stevenson and Bill Sahlman, who have influenced thinking and writing about entrepreneurship for decades, and they both read early versions of the manuscript.

I also want to thank a number of entrepreneurs for their willingness to answer questions that focused on difficulties and even failures rather than success. They include Jeff Bussgang, Janet Kraus, Christopher Michel, Gary Mueller, Gary Rogers, and Jim Sharpe. I also want to thank the other entrepreneurs I interviewed confidentially.

I am grateful to several friends and colleagues for their contributions to this book, which typically involved reading long, early, ungainly drafts of it. Their comments, critiques, and suggestions were very valuable. I am especially indebted to David Garvin, Joshua Margolis, Lynn Paine, Bob Pozen, Clayton Rose, and Sandra Sucher. My daughters, Maria, Luisa, and Gabriella, and my son-in-law, Lee Lockwood, also made many valuable suggestions, as did Michael Duffy. My editor, Melinda Adams Merino, provided practical and insightful guidance from the earliest phases of this project. Finally, three anonymous reviewers chosen by Harvard Business Review Press read a version of the manuscript with a great deal of care and insight, and I have worked hard to be responsive to their critiques.

I am especially indebted to two other people. My friend Ken Winston went far beyond the call of duty and loyalty by reading several drafts of this book over several years, asking many hard questions about what I was really trying to convey, and making many valuable suggestions about how to get ideas and arguments right. Finally, over several years, my wife, Patricia O'Brien, patiently listened to my ideas about this book and read several drafts of it. She provided encouragement, criticism, suggestions, corrections, and many valuable ideas, clearly and concisely stated, all of which added immeasurably to this effort.

Harvard Business School also deserves a great deal of credit. Its generous alumni, particularly John Shad, provided the time and resources that made this work possible. Over several years, I was able to try out some of the ideas in the book in MBA and executive classrooms as well as in informal settings. Deans Jay Light and Nitin Nohria and the heads of the school's Division of Research helped me find the time to pursue this project, and two assistants, Andi Truax and Sean Curran, helped in countless ways to bring this effort to completion.

Despite the generous and thoughtful efforts of everyone I have mentioned, this book no doubt has errors, small and large, and they are my responsibility.

ABOUT THE AUTHOR

JOSEPH BADARACCO is the John Shad Professor of Business Ethics at Harvard Business School, where he teaches in the school's MBA and executive programs. Badaracco is the author of several books on leadership, decision making, and responsibility. These include *Defining Moments: When Managers Must Choose between Right and Right*; *Leading Quietly: An Unorthodox Guide to Doing the Right Thing*; and *Questions of Character: Illuminating the Heart of Leadership through Literature*. These books have been translated into ten languages. Badaracco is a graduate of St. Louis University, Oxford University, where he was a Rhodes scholar, and Harvard Business School, where he earned an MBA and a DBA.